Base Ball in Cincinnati

Base Ball in Cincinnati

A History

by Harry Ellard

McFarland Historical Baseball Library, 3
Gary Mitchem, Marty McGee *and* Mark Durr, *Editors*

McFarland & Company, Inc., Publishers
Jefferson, North Carolina, and London

Frontispiece: Harry Ellard

Library of Congress Cataloguing-in-Publication Data

Ellard, Harry, d. 1913.
　　Base ball in Cincinnati : a history / by Harry Ellard.
　　[Gary Mitchem, Marty McGee and Mark Durr series editors]
　　　　p. cm. — (McFarland historical baseball library ; 3)
　　Originally published: Cincinnati : Press of Johnson & Hardin, 1907.
　　Includes index.

　　ISBN 0-7864-1726-9 (softcover : 50# alkaline paper)

　　1. Baseball. 2. Baseball—Ohio—Cincinnati. I. Title: Baseball in
Cincinnati. II. Title. III. Series.
GV863.O32E44　2004
796.357'09771'78—dc22　　　　　　　　　　　　　　　2003024608

British Library cataloguing data are available

On the cover: The Cincinnati Red Stockings of 1869
(From an original Mathew B. Brady photograph)

Manufactured in the United States of America

McFarland & Company, Inc., Publishers
　Box 611, Jefferson, North Carolina 28640
　　www.mcfarlandpub.com

To HON. AUGUST HERRMANN
this volume is respectfully dedicated

From a recent photo. Hon. August Herrmann,
President, Cincinnati Baseball Club.

From a recent photo. Col. Max C. Fleischmann,
Secretary-Treasurer, Cincinnati Baseball Club.

Preface

During the past few years the history of Cincinnati, with its many business interests and its active connection in all progressive movements, has been faithfully written.

The record of the early pioneers has been graphically described. Events, scenes and incidents have all received their full share of attention from the community, so that nothing pertaining to the honor and glory of Cincinnati, has been neglected.

There is, however, one feature in connection with our local history which has been wholly overlooked, a feature which has carried the name and fame of Cincinnati over the whole country. For it can truly be said that no correct and detailed history of our national game of baseball, which has attracted the attention of thousands of our citizens, has ever been written.

From time to time fragmentary accounts of the origin and progress of baseball, as it existed in our community, have appeared in the papers and magazines, but it has remained to the writer to present for the first time a full and complete history of the game of baseball from its first organization in our midst until the present day.

The author is in possession of many of the books, scores, photographs and documents pertaining to the Cincinnati Baseball Club, especially during the years from 1866 to 1871, to which no one has ever had access, thus enabling him, by the publication of this work, to give to the public the most authentic and complete history ever written concerning the game as played within our city.

For the first time the connected story has been told of all the clubs and games, associating, as it will be seen, the names of many of the prominent men of Cincinnati, both in professional and business life, with the early history of baseball.

The career of the victorious Red Stockings has become a traditional heritage to all lovers of the game. There is scarcely an enthusiast, young or old, who does not dwell with pride upon this record of unparalleled success, which has never been equaled, and the achievements of the old Red Stockings of 1869 will always act as a stimulus to the present players to approach the high standard once established for the game.

The author desires to thank many of the old members of the Cincinnati Baseball Club, during the years previous to 1871, for much valuable information they have given him, and for the great interest they have manifested in the writing of this book.

Contents

Contents

Adoption of the First Uniforms of the Club.
Short Trousers Inaugurated.
The Cincinnati Juniors Figured.
Youngsters in All Our Suburbs Had Good Nines.
Baseball Clubs in Cincinnati in 1868.
Harry Wright Married.
Indians Play on Cincinnati Ball Grounds.
Charter Roll of Membership of the Original Cincinnati Baseball
   Club.
Scores Made by the Cincinnati Baseball Club in 1868.
Scores Made by the Buckeye Baseball Club in 1868.

The Famous Reds of 1869 and Their Victories.
Were the First Professional Team in the Country.
Players Were Secured by a Cincinnatian from All Parts of the
   Country.
Never Defeated.
Detailed Account of Each Player.
Salary List.
Their Eastern Tour.
The Great Game with the Mutuals of New York City.

The Unbeaten Redlegs of 1869.
Great Reception upon Their Return Home.
Most Famous of Ballplayers.
Their Western Tour.
The Reds of Sixty-nine.
Official Scores for the Season.

The Cincinnati Baseball Club of 1870.
The Players of the Year.

Contents

Contents

Editors' Note

Harry Ellard's *Base Ball in Cincinnati* was originally published in 1907, by the author, and made available by subscription. Motivated in part by recent books on Cincinnati history that "wholly overlooked" baseball, Ellard drew on family connections and his own large collection of local baseball books, records, and memorabilia to write the story of baseball in his home town. It was a public gesture of civic—and, it turns out, familial—pride not uncommon among the upper class at the turn of the century, but one that provided later baseball historians with an early, detailed account of the first openly professional baseball team.

Ellard's connections to Cincinnati baseball were close. His father, sporting goods retailer George B. Ellard, was one of the original members of the Cincinnati Baseball Club in 1866, credited by some as the first Cincinnati player to wear red stockings. By 1869, George Ellard was off the field, but continued to work with president Aaron Champion and manager Harry Wright to acquire players for the unbeaten 1869 team, and his company manufactured the baseball—called the "Ellard Ball"—used by the club. George's other son, John V., also had ties to the club, playing for at least three years with the junior nines first organized in 1867 by club member John Draper.

Little is known about the author himself. His obituary indicates that he was 54 when he died in 1913. It's believed that beginning in 1895, he lived for 10 years in or around Denver, Colorado, where he was sent by his parents to recover from tuberculosis. While there, in 1899, he published a collection of poems about frontier life titled *Ranch Tales of the Rockies*. Interestingly, it is by that book that his obituary identifies him, saying of Ellard that "Harry G. Ellard ... was better known to the literary world as the 'Cowboy Poet' and the 'Poet Lariat.'"

Ellard has been described by recent historians as a "Cincinnati baseball writer," which seems to point tentatively back at *Base Ball in Cincinnati*, and as a "sportswriter" or "scribe," terms most commonly reserved for sports journalists. But the evidence is lacking. A serially published article on the 1869 Red Stockings—heavily drawn from by one of the local histories Ellard refers to in his preface—was published in 1902 by the *Cincinnati Commercial*. Much of it was run verbatim in chapters 10 and 11 of *Base Ball in Cincinnati*. The only other writings known to be Ellard's are collected in a scrapbook at the Denver Public Library. They were locally published pieces about frontier life.

Whatever Ellard's profession or baseball expertise, he was resourceful. The fullness of his coverage for the Red Stockings tours of 1868, 1869, and 1870 is a big reason that *Base Ball in Cincinnati* turns up in the bibliographies of new books. But it might be the chapters on the local amateur scene that most impress. Ellard is able to provide the organization dates, the names of starting and sometimes second nines, match scores, and even the names of club board members. Special attention is given the Live Oak and Buckeye clubs, the great local rivals of the early Red Stockings. These rich middle chapters are introduced by a brief general history of the game and followed by a discussion of baseball in the city from 1876 through September of 1907.

This last "chapter" represents a structural curiosity. Just after Chapter IX, which the Table of Contents indicates is penultimate, the reader encounters a foreword. In it Ellard announces that the book's final section—two chapters that cover Cincinnati baseball after 1876 and the establishment of the National League—has been contributed by Ren Mulford, a local baseball editor and correspondent for Francis Richter's *Sporting Life*. The book also contains at least one stylistic inconsistency of note: *baseball* is treated in the title as two words, after the early style, and nearly everywhere else as one.

The text of the McFarland Historical Baseball Library edition comes from the book as it was published in 1908, expanded by 26 pages (from 249 to 277) beyond the 1907 subscription edition. The pagination has been adjusted to fit series specifications, and three facsimile signatures—Ellard's below the Frontispiece and then with the Foreword to Munford's chapters, Munford's below his portrait in that section—have been dropped. With only minor exceptions, the text is otherwise unaltered from the original. An index and this note have been added, and several photos have been re-sized, their placement slightly adjusted. The chapter number and running heads have been added to Chapter 10; they were omitted from the 1908 edition, presumably by mistake. Finally, the Table of Contents, which included the number for Chapter 10 but failed to indicate the presence of Chapter 11, has also been corrected.

The Editors

Baseball in Cincinnati
A History

CHAPTER I

History of Our National Game of Baseball—Cincinnati Was Always a Stronghold for Fans.

Probably no athletic game has gained greater prominence in the United States than that of baseball. Although many claim it is of English origin, still I am convinced that the game is strictly American, being an evolution of the old game called "Cat Ball," or what was known in some parts of New England as "Two Old Cat."

Other athletic games have come forth from time to time, in which great interest has been taken, but their lives have been of short duration and they soon sank almost into oblivion; but baseball still remains, and there is every indication that it will survive for many years to come.

Rounders was begun in the early '30s in England, as a pastime for healthy outdoor exercise both for men and boys, and was introduced into this country about 1840. In order to give my readers an idea of what the game was, I quote from an old English work on outdoor sports a description of the game as it was played in the early part of the last century. It will be plainly seen that it is but the merest outline of what is now known as the great national game:

"ROUNDERS.—This game is played with a ball and bats, or sticks, something the form of a policeman's truncheon. A hole is first made about a foot across and half a foot deep. Four other stations are

marked with pegs stuck in the ground, topped with a piece of paper, so as to be readily seen. Sides are then chosen, one of which goes in. Suppose that there are five players, yet more can play on each side, to start the game. One player on the side that is out stands in the middle of the five-sided space, and pitches the ball toward the middle of the hole. He is called the feeder. The batsman hits it off, if he can; in which case he drops the stick and runs to the nearest station, thence to the third, and all around if the hit has been a far one. The other side are scouting and trying to put him out, either by hitting the batsman as he is running or by sending the ball into the hole, which is called grounding. The player at the hole may decline to strike the ball, but if he hits at it and misses twice running he is out. When a player makes the round of the stations back to the hole, his side counts one toward the game. When all the players are out, either by being hit or the ball being grounded, the other side get their innings. When there are only two players left, a chance is given to prolong the innings by one of them getting three balls from the feeder, and if he can give a hit such as to enable him to run the whole round, all his side come in again and the counting is resumed. The feeder is generally the best player on his side, much depending on his skill and art. The scouts should seldom aim at the runners from a distance, but throw the ball up to the feeder or to some one near, who will try to hit or to ground, as seems the most advisable. A caught ball also puts the runner out."

TOWNBALL IN AMERICA.

The first townball club organized in this country of which we have any record, was known as the Olympic Ball Club, which was

Opposite: **A real old-time baseball game during the fifties. Note the position and dignity of the umpire.**

organized in Philadelphia on July 4, 1833, and was established by the union of two associations of Townball Players. One of these organizations began playing at Camden, N.J., as early as the spring of 1831. On the first day there were but four players who joined in the game "Cat Ball" or "Two Old Cat" as mentioned above.

When this association of ball players was organized it had no constitution or by-laws, or elected members, but the absence of these formalities was not felt, and was no disadvantage, for there were no quarrels or disputes among the players, who always found the principles of good-fellowship and gentlemanly intercourse a sufficient rule for their guidance.

KNICKERBOCKER WAS FIRST CLUB.

To get at the origin of baseball in America it will be necessary for us to go back to the pioneer club of the country. It has been conceded by all who have studied the history of baseball that the Knickerbocker Club, of New York, organized September 23, 1845, was the first.

There was, however, a club called the New York Club, which existed before the Knickerbocker, but we shall not be far wrong if we award to the latter club the honor of being the pioneer of the present game of baseball.

Before the organization of this club the rule of play in reference to putting a player out was to throw the ball at him and hit him, but, owing to the fact that this practice resulted in some very severe accidents, the rules were changed to placing men on bases and making it requisite for a player to be touched by the ball while in the hands of his adversary.

To Mr. Alexander J. Cartwright is credited the formation of the

Knickerbocker Club. He was quite an enthusiast in the old game and he soon gathered around him a number of faithful followers. One day upon the field he proposed the organization of a permanent regular club to several devotees of the game; so on the date which we mention above, the Knickerbocker Baseball Club was formed with the following officers: President, Duncan F. Curry; Vice-President, William R. Wheaton; Secretary and Treasurer, William Tucker. It was thus that these gentlemen formed an organization which was the nucleus of the now great American game. As Mr. Alexander J. Cartwright conceived the idea of the formation of the first baseball club in America, he is certainly deserving of the title "Father of Baseball."

The Knickerbockers played their first match game on June 19, 1846, with a party of New York gentlemen who styled themselves the "New York Club," but who had no permanent organization. Only four innings were played; the game in those days being determined in favor of the side that made the first twenty-one runs. The score stood: New York, 23; Knickerbockers, 1. The first uniform of the club was adopted at a meeting held April 24, 1849. This consisted of blue woolen pants, white flannel shirts and straw hats.

The following are the first regular rules of baseball of which we have any record. They are those adopted by the Knickerbocker Club in 1845. These rules were in vogue until the formation of the national Association of Baseball Players in 1857:

FIRST RULES OF BASEBALL.

Section 1. The bases shall be from "home" to second base forty-two paces; from first to third base forty-two paces equi-distant.

Sec. 2. The game to consist of twenty-one counts or aces, but at the conclusion an equal number of hands must be played.

Sec. 3. The ball must be pitched and not thrown for the bat.

Sec. 4. A ball knocked outside the range of the first base or third base is foul.

Sec. 5. Three balls being struck at and missed, and the last one caught, is considered fair and the striker is bound to run.

Sec. 6. A ball being struck or tipped and caught either flying or on the first bound, is a hand out.

Sec. 7. A player running the bases shall be out if a ball is in the hands of an adversary on the base, or the runner is touched by it before he makes his base, it being understood, however, that in no instance is a ball to be thrown at him.

Sec. 8. A player running, who shall prevent an adversary from catching or getting the ball before making his base, is out.

Sec. 9. If two hands are already out, a player running home at the time a ball is struck can not make an ace if the striker is caught out.

Sec. 10. Three hands out, all out.

Sec. 11. Players must take their strikes in regular turn.

Sec. 12. No ace or base can be made on a foul strike.

Sec. 13. A runner can not be put out in making one base when a balk is made by the pitcher.

Sec. 14. But one base allowed when the ball bounds out of the field when struck.

All those who are familiar with the rules of the present day will at once see the great difference between the game as played then and that which is now the attractive feature of American sports.

The Knickerbocker Club had its grounds on what was then known as the Elysian Fields, and so successful was it there in arousing interest in the game that the formation of other clubs soon followed.

Opposite: **A baseball game in full swing during the early sixties. Note the position of the catcher while runner is stealing second.**

The next club formed was the Gotham Baseball Club, organized in March, 1852, with Mr. Tuche as President. It was then that the Knickerbockers had their first rivals, and many were the interesting contests between them. On June 30, 1854, was played one of the greatest games, in which the Knickerbockers suffered their first defeat, on the Gotham grounds, Red House, Harlem. The game lasted three hours and sixteen innings were played, resulting in a score of 21 to 16, in favor of the Gothams.

The Eagle Baseball Club, of New York, was the third one to spring into existence, organized in April of 1854, and among its founders are the names of John W. Mott and William C. Conner. The Empire Club, of New York, organized October 23, 1854, is fourth on the list, with thirteen members. This supposed unlucky number, however, had the opposite effect upon them, for their success in the field in these first years of baseball is well known.

The position of umpire was a dignified one in the early days. The man occupying it seemed to be perfectly conscious of the honor conferred upon him in being assigned to this office, not less, in his estimation, to one of high political importance.

He donned Prince Albert coat, silk hat and cane, and often wore long, flowing side whiskers. His position on the field was between home plate and first base, given a stool on which to rest one foot as he viewed the game. He gave his decisions deliberately, for the action of the game was not as rapid as at the present time. The swift manner in which baseball is played now would scarcely demand the services of so dignified a judge.

The scorer's position on the field was about twenty feet to the right of the catcher. He was given a large table and plenty of paper, and inasmuch as refreshments, both liquid and solid, were served at every game, the scorer came in for a full share, and fare sumptuously.

The following is a list of the charter clubs of the association, who were represented at the first convention, with the date of organization and the location of the grounds of each:

CLUB	ORGANIZED	LOCATION OF GROUNDS
Knickerbocker	September 23, 1845	Hoboken.
Gotham	March, 1852	Hoboken.
Eagle	April, 1854	Hoboken.
Empire	October 23, 1854	Hoboken.
Excelsior	December 8, 1854	South Brooklyn.
Putnam	May, 1855	Williamsburgh.
Newark	May 1, 1855	Newark.
Baltic	June 4, 1855	New York.
Eckford	July, 1855	Brooklyn.
Eckford	June 27, 1855	Greenpoint.
Union	July 17, 1855	Morrisania.
Continental	October, 1855	Williamsburgh.
Atlantic	August 14, 1855	Brooklyn.
Atlantic	August, 1855	Jamaica, L.I.
Harlem	March, 1856	New York
Enterprise	June 28, 1856	Bedford.
Atlantic	August 14, 1856	Bedford.
Star	October, 1856	South Brooklyn.
Independent	January, 1857	New York.
Liberty	March 1, 1857	New Brunswick, N.J.
Metropolitan	March 4, 1857	New York.
Champion	March 14, 1857	New York.
Hamilton	March 23, 1857	Brooklyn.
St. Nicholas	April 28, 1857	Hoboken.

As will be seen from the above record, the years 1855 and 1856 were prolific of new clubs, and, of course, a great number of exciting contests took place, the result of which was the creation of a thorough furor for the game, and the manifestation of a great degree of interest in the welfare and progress of this manly pastime by the rapidly increasing numbers of the advocates of outdoor sports.

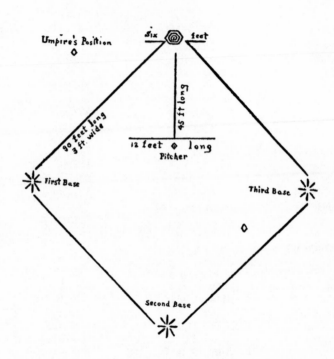

Scorer's Position ◊

Catcher ◊

Umpire's Position ◊

six | feet

45 ft long

90 feet long
3 ft. wide

12 feet ◊ long
Pitcher

First Base ✳

Third Base ✳

◊

Second Base
✳

Right ◊ Field

Left ◊ Field

Centre ◆ Field

Diagram of a baseball field. 1859.

◆ 14 ◆

The enthusiasm over the victories of the year 1855 and 1856 seemed to give a new impetus to baseball. Interest was widespread, new clubs were organized, which created a spirit of emulation and rivalry, which led to many well-contested matches between the different clubs. The game now appears to have had such a strong hold upon the community that it was deemed advisable at this time to revise the rules to meet in some respects the new conditions which had now arisen. For this purpose the different clubs held preliminary meetings, and it was finally decided to hold a convention, in which delegates from each State would be present. Consequently, the call was issued by the Knickerbocker Club, and the first convention was held in New York City in May of 1857, when was formed the National Association of Baseball Players.

The rules and regulations for governing the game were revised and amended at the second meeting of this association, held at Cooper Institute, March 9, 1859. Many important changes were made and a new code was established. At this time it was decided to abolish refreshments in connection with the matches. This custom, which was originally intended to create friendly feeling between participants in the game, finally became a very extravagant exhibition of emulation between the clubs, each one striving to excel the other in the quantity and quality of the feast presented. As these elaborate refreshments seemed unnecessary to the welfare of the game, it was considered prudent to discontinue them altogether.

Formed State Association.

They also formed State associations, so that each year delegates were sent to the annual convention by each State belonging. In 1857 there were sixteen clubs enrolled, in 1858 twenty-nine clubs, in 1859 forty-nine clubs, in 1860 sixty-two clubs, and in 1861 thirty-four clubs. As the war broke out in 1861, which took many of the active young men to the front, interest in baseball ceased to a great extent.

In these dark days of the Union, baseball was a minor consideration and many clubs were disbanded, so that the membership in the association dropped off considerably in the years of 1861-'62-'63-'64. When the war was over, new clubs were formed, and at the convention of 1865 there were ninety-one clubs represented.

The tenth annual convention of the National Association of Baseball Players was held at Clinton Hall, New York, December 12, 1866, with 202 clubs represented. Dr. John Draper, of Cincinnati, was delegate from Ohio to this convention, representing the Live Oak Club, as was also Mr. Philip Lishawa, representing the Buckeye Club. Clubs from Oregon, in the West, to Maine, in the East; Missouri, Tennessee and Virginia, in the South, to Vermont, in the North, sent delegates to this convention, and the flattering reception given them as their names were announced, and especially the applause which greeted the Southern clubs, afforded ample proof of the truly conservative feeling which prevailed at this convention.

The bitter sectional feeling between the North and the South was quite strong at this time. It had been difficult to subdue the antagonism which had been engendered by the war, but it is well worthy of comment to mention the influence exerted by a manly sport as a means of reconciling these diverse factions. When it came to a game of baseball, all difference of opinion was laid aside. Fraternal feeling was uppermost, old political scores were forgotten in the attempt of each club to make a record score for itself, and it is pleasant to note that the applause and cheers were never stronger than when the name of one of the Southern delegates was proposed as a candidate for the presidency of the Association.

The Introduction of
Townball into Cincinnati.

Townball, from which baseball is an evolution, was first introduced into Cincinnati in 1860. This game is played on a field with
bases marked at about one-half the distance of baseball. A short bat,
which is used with one hand only, was employed in knocking a ball
that was much smaller and much softer than a baseball. Four innings
only were played, and the number playing on each side could vary from
ten to fifteen. The scores ranged about the same as early baseball, yet
in looking over the old score-book of games of townball played in
Cincinnati during the war, we find one of 146 to 21. This game was
played here by a number of school-teachers and their friends upon
a lot upon which the Cincinnati Hospital now stands. The Hospital then was a small building at one end, and frequently the young
interns would join in the game. Among them are recalled the names
of Dr. Williams, the oculist, Dr. Cilley, and Dr. McKenzie.

Although not regularly organized, these old players called
themselves the Excelsior Townball Club. They played under this
name for three years. In 1861 they obtained permission from the City
Council to play in the Orphan Asylum lot, on Elm Street, where the
Music Hall was afterwards erected.

At the suggestion of Geo. F. Sands, one of the prominent members of this club, a meeting was called at the office of Luke Kent,
the jeweler, at Main and Fourth Streets, for the purpose of estab-
lishing the club upon a permanent basis.

Sands Was Elected President.

As a result, the Cincinnati Buckeye Townball Club was organized
October 1, 1863, with George F. Sands as President; James Sherwood,

Vice-President; Frank Harvey, Secretary; John B. Sheidemantle, Treasurer. Among the members at that time were John B. Sheidemantle, George W. Smith, James E. Sherwood, B.O.M. DeBeck, Jesse DeBeck, W.D. Gibson, Charles Gould, Samuel Hughes, George Wehmer, W.J. Ogden, Eugene Hammett, Ben Brookshaw, Charles Jones and others.

Later on they secured grounds in the Millcreek bottoms, just north of Lincoln Park, where are now located the buildings of the American Oak Leather Company, which were afterward fenced in and a clubhouse and seats erected. Under the name of the "Cincinnati Buckeye Townball Club" games were played until the fall of 1866, when the club was re-organized and henceforth

From an old portrait made at the time. George F. Sands, *President* Buckeye Townball Club, 1863. *President* National Association of Baseball Players, 1867.

was known as the "Buckeye Baseball Club." New members were added. Among them were Charles F. Wilstach, then Mayor; Harry Tatem, John F. Wiltsee, Steven Faulkner. The players which constituted the Buckeye Baseball Club nine in 1866 were:

William H. Boake	Center Field
James E. Sherwood	Catcher
Charles H. Gould	First Base
George F. Sands	Second Base

B.O.M. DeBeck .... Third Base
John L. Boake .... Left Field
John B. Shiedemantle .... Shortstop
George W. Smith .... Pitcher
George P. Miller .... Right Field

During the baseball period of the club John G. Shiedemantle was considered one of the best players, and much of the success of a game was dependent upon him. If one was unfortunately lost during his absence, the club members consoled themselves in the face of their defeat, by saying to the victors, "You just wait until 'Sheiddy' comes home, then the tables will turn."

The Buckeye nine of 1867 had the following players:

William H. Skiff .... Catcher
George W. Smith .... Pitcher
John B. Shiedemantle .... Shortstop
Charles H. Gould .... First Base
William Wright .... Second Base
Thomas Tallow .... Third Base
John Meagher .... Right Field
William H. Boake .... Center Field
John L. Boake .... Left Field

Through the efforts of Matthew M. Yorston, the first baseball club in Cincinnati was formed. So unknown were baseballs in that time that Mr. Yorston made with his own hands the first ball ever used by the club, which began to play in the fall of 1860. This club played baseball, and sometimes townball, all through the war, and among its members were Dr. John Draper, Octavius Tudor, John C. Davis, Matt Yorston, James Fogerty, Theodore Frost, J.R. Brockway and others. This club at one time played on grounds at the foot

Right: **From a recent photo. Matthew M. Yorston,** *Organizer* **First Baseball Club in Cincinnati, 1860.**

of Eighth Street, near the site where the factory of the Crane & Breed Manufacturing Company now stands, and at another time on the old potter's field where is now Lincoln Park. The increase in membership after the war led them to form a regular organization, and the club was then called the Live Oak Baseball Club, which was really the first baseball club here.

ORGANIZATION OF THE
LIVE OAK BASEBALL CLUB.

The Live Oak Baseball Club was organized at a called meeting on Thursday evening, July 15, 1866, when the following officers were elected for the first year: John C. Davis, President; R.B. Lee, Vice-President; E. McCammon, Secretary; C. McCammon, Treasurer.

The directors of the club were: M.M. Yorston, T.C. Frost, Dr. John Draper.

The first match game of baseball ever played in Cincinnati was played by this club on September 8, 1866, with the Eagle Baseball Club, then located across the river in a place known as Brooklyn, Ky., which was near Dayton. The members of the teams were as follows:

Chapter I

LIVE OAK BASEBALL CLUB.

Dr. John Draper .... Catcher and Captain
T.C. Frost .... Pitcher
D.R. Powers .... First Base
Si Hicks .... Second Base
James Fogarty .... Third Base
R.B. Lee .... Right Field
J. Hicks .... Center Field
John R. Brockway .... Left Field
M.M. Yorston .... Shortstop

EAGLE BASEBALL CLUB.

Mahaffey .... Catcher and Captain
Pudder .... Pitcher
Lyford .... First Base
Bricker .... Second Base
Southard .... Third Base
Kennedy .... Right Field
Lusk .... Center Field
Ford .... Left Field
Swift .... Shortstop

The scorers of the game were J.W. Rorer and Washington T. Porter. Mahaffey, the catcher for the Eagles, was one of the strongest batters that ever hit a ball. He used only one hand and a short bat eighteen inches long.

This game was full of excitement and interest, notwithstanding the great discrepancy in runs. It ended with a score of 52 to 12 in favor of the Live Oak Club, which took the ball that was played with during the game, as a trophy. This was the custom during these early days of baseball matches.

The next game was played by the Live Oak Club on September

From a recent photo. John C. Davis, *President* Live Oak Baseball Club, 1866.

15, 1866, when they were matched against the Covington Baseball Club. This was the first game ever played in Covington, Ky., and it was played near the residence of B.W. Foley. The Covington Club was composed of the following players:

B.W. Foley ..... Catcher and Captain
Matthews .... Pitcher
Bertie .... First Base
Moses Grant .... Second Base
W.L. Porter .... Third Base
Thomas Fallon .... Right Field
W. Grant .... Center Field
Parker .... Left Field
Ben. Brookshaw .... Shortstop
Holmes Hoge was the umpire.

This game saw the defeat of the Live Oak Club in a score of 28 to 21 in favor of the Covington Club, which captured the ball as the trophy of the day. One of the old rules in vogue at this time was that if a ball was knocked over the fence only one base was allowed.

♦ CHAPTER II ♦

How the First Cincinnati Baseball Club Was Organized—The Great Baseball Tournament of 1867—Scores of 1866 and 1867.

Baseball is a sport which has always had the support and encouragement of our best men, and the people of Cincinnati look back with much pride to the days of the old Red Stockings, when such men as Sir Alfred T. Goshorn, Aaron B. Champion, Hon. Bellamy Storer, Judge Nicholas Longworth, Judge William Worthington, United States Justice Stanley Matthews, General Andrew Hickenlooper, Drausin Wulsin, George B. Ellard, H.C. Yergason, John R. McLean, W. Austin Goodman, A. Howard Hinkle, Theodore Cook, and many others of our leading citizens, took an active interest in the game; when the leaders of society among our women also attended and applauded our victorious champions in the field when the prominent matches were played. The memory of the old Red Stocking days is a tender recollection in the hearts of many. In recalling the incidents of that time the voices of the veterans who belonged to this famous club speak with enthusiasm and pride, their countenances beam with pleasure, and their hearts seem lighter, when dwelling on the glory of baseball in the days of the past.

The organization and first meeting of the Cincinnati Baseball Club was held July 23, 1866, in the law office of Tilden, Sherman & Moulton, which was then in the old Selves Building, No. 17½ West

Third Street. There were present Aaron B. Champion, Alfred T. Goshorn, Henry Glassford, William Tilden, George B. Ellard, J. William Johnson, Holmes Hoge, Quinton Corwine and a few others. A suitable constitution and by-laws were adopted and an election of officers took place, resulting in the election of Alfred T. Goshorn, President; Aaron B. Champion, Vice-President; Henry Glassford, Secretary; E.E. Townley, Treasurer. The office of scorer was not filled until the following year, 1867, when William Worthington was chosen as first scorer and George B. Ellard as manager. The name given to the club at first was the Resolutes, but it was soon changed to that of the Cincinnati Baseball Club, at the suggestion of J. William Johnson, who was also instrumental in calling the first meeting.

The club at this time was composed mostly of members of the bar, many of whom were Yale and Harvard graduates in the latter '50s and the early '60s, and some of these later in life filled positions of the highest honor and trust in official life. Among the active and enthusiastic players on the diamond at many of the early matches played were Bellamy Storer, J. William Johnson, John R. McLean, J. Wayne Neff, Samuel Kemper, John C. How, Charles E. Callahan, George B. Ellard, Holmes Hoge and O.H. Tudor. In the practice games were to be seen Drausin Wulsin, Quinton Corwine, Billy Caldwell, J.M. Kennedy, Stanley Matthews, Andrew Hickenlooper and others.

The club had its grounds at first at the foot of Ninth Street, in the Millcreek bottoms, and it was here the inaugural matches were played. In 1867 the club moved to the grounds of the Union Cricket Club, with which was made a quasi alliance. These grounds were situated at the foot of Richmond Street. They were used in the summer for cricket and baseball and in winter were flooded and used for skating purposes, where great enthusiasm was manifested in this winter sport, with a series of interesting carnivals.

Alfred T. Goshorn, *President*   **Aaron B. Champion,** *Vice-President*

Henry Glassford, *Treasurer*   **Edward E. Townley,** *Secretary*

First Officers Cincinnati Baseball Club, 1866. From photos taken at the time.

Base Ball in Cincinnati

The Union Cricket Club had been in existence since October, 1856, and its officers in 1867 were: President, George B. Ellard; Vice-President, I. Burnet Resor; Secretary, William Resor, Jr.; Treasurer, Benjamin F. Wright, and Harry Wright, property man. Upon the removal of the Cincinnati Baseball Club to the grounds of the Union Cricket Club, a great number of the cricket club members became members of the baseball club, and by this means the team was greatly strengthened and interest in baseball gained a new impetus.

Harry Wright, so well known in baseball circles in the early days, was previous to his coming to Cincinnati the bowler for the New York Cricket Club, working only during the summer at $12 per week, and at his trade (that of jeweler) during the winter, but in August, 1865, he was engaged by George B. Ellard, at a salary of $1,200 a year, to play in the same capacity for the Union Cricket Club, which position he held until November 22, 1867, when he was engaged to act as pitcher for the baseball club at the same salary. He had, however, played baseball in the East, with the Knickerbockers and the Excelsiors, but had retired from these clubs, as cricket was his favorite pastime.

Owing to the increasing membership in the club, it was found necessary to construct a large clubhouse to accommodate the men. At a meeting held at the office of George B. Ellard, April 3, 1867, plans of the building intended to be erected were submitted by Duncan & Bunten, the old contractors and builders on Freeman Avenue. These plans were accepted and the new building erected at a cost of $2,400, with an additional expense of $1,350 for a more substantial fence around the grounds.

At a meeting held at the office of Geo. B. Ellard, on June 12, 1867, there were present Messrs. Wm. Resor, H.A. Glassford, D. Schwartz, Drausin Wulsin, Ben. F. Wright and Geo. B. Ellard. It was resolved that the members of the Cincinnati Baseball Club and the Union Cricket Club be admitted free to all matches, also that the rates of admission be fixed at ten cents for home matches and twenty-five cents for foreign matches. Ladies free.

On September 10 following, it was resolved that thereafter the charge for admission to the grounds on the occasion of all matches should be twenty-five cents and that ladies be charged the same as gentlemen. No disreputable characters were allowed on the grounds. The audience behaved themselves, and did not insult umpires or players.

We also notice among the rules and regulations of the club that "no ardent spirits shall be kept for sale on the grounds," yet in looking over some of the old bills presented to the club we find one from the caterer, where the item "drinks and lemons for the policemen" is mentioned several times, at a cost ranging from forty-five cents to $1.75.

LIVE OAKS AND BUCKEYES RIVALS.

The great early local rivals of the Cincinnati Baseball Club were the Live Oaks and the Buckeyes. Many were the matches played with these two clubs, solely for the honor and glory of the victory and the exercise, enjoyment and friendly feeling which the game engendered.

In recalling the games of this time, one was played with the Buckeye Club. James Sherwood, afterwards a teacher in the public schools, was at the bat. He succeeded in reaching first base very nicely. He then became so interested in the next man's play that when the ball was struck he forgot to run to second, thus putting both men out.

Another notable game was with the Indianapolis Club. A dispute arose in regard to the catching of a ball by John R. McLean, who was acting as catcher at that time for the Cincinnati Club. A Mr. Sharkey, catcher for the Indianapolis nine, had the temerity to shake his finger in the face of Mr. McLean, who was then in prime athletic condition. Seeing the kind of material he had run against, Mr. Sharkey thought discretion the better part of valor and allowed Mr. McLean's opinion to stand without further argument. Mr. McLean was the first man to catch close behind the bat, with bare hands. In those days masks, gloves and protectors were unknown, and the catching of a ball in this manner was exceedingly dangerous.

From a recent photo. Hon. John R. McLean, *Catcher* Cincinnati Baseball Team, 1867.

On June 20, 1867, the Cincinnati Club went to Louisville, at the invitation of the club of that city, to play a match game with it. The Louisvilles were quite confident of victory, but the game ended in their defeat by a score of 42 to 19.

In returning from Louisville a banquet was held on the boat to celebrate the victory. At the same time a number of ladies were on the same boat, and the mind of the captain was very much exercised lest the exuberant spirits of the victors would disturb his fair passengers, and he made the request that there should be no undue noise or hilarity. With gentlemanly sense of honor, the victorious Red Stockings promised faithfully that the strictest decorum should be observed. This banquet stands on record as being the most unique, as well as the most silent one, ever celebrated. Voices were modulated to the lowest tone when toasts were proposed, no clinking glasses gave forth a sound, while "Hip, hip, hurrah!" was uttered in the most quiet manner. Champagne flowed freely, but the remarkable repression of ebullition of feeling among the Red Stockings seemed to temper the effect. The captain afterward made the remark that it was the stillest party he ever saw, where so much wine was present.

The return match to this victory was played on July 4 on the grounds in Cincinnati. The Louisville Club chartered a boat, bringing with it some fifty or sixty ladies, who occupied seats in the "Grand Duchess," now called the grand stand.

LOUISVILLE WAS DISAPPOINTED.

The Louisvilles had promised their fair companions that a signal victory awaited them; that the ignominious defeat of the Reds would result. Alas for prophetic utterances! The Cincinnati Club was again triumphant by a score of 60 to 24, but, nevertheless, some hearts were conquered by the bewitching glances from the eyes of the pretty Kentucky women.

The only game lost by the Cincinnati Club in 1867 out of the eighteen played was on July 15, to the Nationals, of Washington, with a score of 53 to 10 in favor of the Nationals. On July 11 it had a match with the Live Oak Club, to prepare for the coming contest with the Nationals. An accident occurred in this game; otherwise the score would have been different.

John R. McLean was catching for the Cincinnatis, and he was

without an equal in his day. A foul tip on the ball from the bat of one of the players struck Mr. McLean squarely in the eye, closing it for some time. When he returned home his fond mother was so grieved by the changed appearance of her boy that she forbade him taking part in another game of baseball, and consequently this was his last appearance on the field for some time.

THE HOLT BASEBALL CLUB, OF NEWPORT, KY.

The game of September 12, of this year, with the Holts, of Newport, was played with a score of 109 to 15 in favor of the Cincinnati Club. In this game John C. How, then acting at first base, made fourteen runs and no outs, seven of the runs being home runs. Harry Wright also made seven home runs. In this game a man who did not make a home run was considered rather a poor player.

Our friends across the river (the Holts, of Newport, Ky.) had the following players on their two nines:

Prather	Catcher
Ferris	Pitcher
Smith	Shortstop
Payne	First Base
Grant	Second Base
Turner	Third Base
Seddens	Right Field
Richardson	Left Field
Buchanan	Center Field

The other nine consisted of the following:

James Ryan .... Catcher
J. Ashby .... Pitcher
John Howe .... Shortstop
A. Seddens .... First Base
G. Berry .... Second Base
G. Creighton .... Third Base
R. Conklin .... Right Field
James Root .... Left Field
G. Nealeaus .... Center Field

So popular was baseball in these early days that parents, their children and grandchildren and entire families would turn out to attend the games. At every game there were private conveyances by the score, a special place being provided for them on the grounds. Every seat would be taken, while ropes were stretched around the spectators on the outfield.

From photo taken at the time. George B. Ellard, *Right Fielder* **Cincinnati Baseball Team, 1867.**

THE ELEVENTH NATIONAL MEET.

On December 11 and 12, 1867, the eleventh annual meeting of the National Association of Baseball Players was held in Philadelphia. The delegates to this convention were men of influence and position in the community and gentlemen in the true sense of the word. From this fact it could be easily seen that baseball as a game had so increased in popularity as to gain the co-operation and support of men well worthy to be at the head of any legislative organization of the country.

It was at this convention that E.H. Greggs, of Chicago, delegate from Illinois, representing fifty-seven clubs, proposed the name of George F. Sands, President of the Buckeye Baseball Club of Cincinnati and delegate from Ohio, representing forty clubs, as President. This nomination was indorsed by the New York delegates, and Mr. Sands was unanimously elected. This was the first time that a Western man had held that position. The honor conferred upon Mr. Sands was greatly appreciated by his friends in Cincinnati, who determined to give him a royal welcome upon his return home. Consequently, upon his arrival he was met at the depot by members of the Cincinnati Buckeye and Live Oak Clubs. These clubs, led by Currier's Band, escorted the honored President to the hotel, to the airs of "Hail to the Chief" and "Johnny Comes Marching Home Again." A reception and sumptuous banquet followed, and toasts, merriment and good feeling prevailed.

MR. SANDS RECEIVED GOLD MEDAL.

It was indeed a jolly evening, which the surviving members of the clubs represented recall with pleasure and delight. Later on Mr. Sands was presented with a handsome gold medal by his club in honor of the occasion. Although his silver hair today (1907) indicates that age has crept upon him, yet, as the veteran principal of the Third Intermediate School, in spirit and in feeling he is as young as in the halcyon days of baseball.

The Cincinnati nine of 1866 was composed of the following players:

Holmes Hoge was captain,
Harry Wright,
Geo. B. Ellard,
J. Con. How,
J. William Johnson,
Chas. A. Callahan,
C. Calvert,
Sam. Kemper,
Aaron B. Champion.

The Union Grounds back of Lincoln Park, which had been leased by the club, were opened July 1, 1867, with a game between the Cincinnati and the Louisville Clubs. It was the first game in this city at which the general public attended, an admission fee was charged, or a newspaper reporter wrote up the game. The first admission ticket ever used for a baseball game in Cincinnati was sold and taken in by Henry T. Lloyd and Henry J. Lloyd on this day.

At this time small silver coins were very scarce and seldom seen. The money taken in at the gate was nearly all in the old ten, fifteen, twenty-five and fifty cent paper currency, or "shin-plasters," as they were called, and it required several hours to count the receipts, which had been thrown in a barrel provided to contain the great number of small bills received.

The regular nine of 1867 was composed of the following players:

John R. McLean .... Catcher
Bellamy Storer .... Second Base
John Con. How .... Shortstop
J. Wayne Neff .... First Base
Moses Grant .... Left Field
Dave Schwartz .... Third Base

Base Ball in Cincinnati

J. William Johnson .... Center Field
Harry Wright .... Pitcher
George B. Ellard .... Right Field
William Worthington .... Scorer

When any of the above players could not be on hand for the game, among the other boys on the field could be found W. Austin Goodman, Drausin Wulsin, the great shortstop of his day, Samuel Kemper, Nicholas Longworth, Lucien Wulsin, H.C. Yergason, an excellent player in his time, and others. Mr. Yergason when at Yale College was a member of the Charter Oak Baseball Club, of Hartford, Conn., playing shortstop in that nine.

From photo taken at the time.
William Worthington, *Scorer*
Cincinnati Baseball Club, 1867.

During these early days of baseball many of the members of the Cincinnati Club were unable to spare the time from their business to play every day during the afternoons. In order to obtain the exhilarating exercise of the game, many would frequently get up at four o'clock in the morning, dress in their baseball outfits, and go down to play a game before breakfast. When reaching the grounds they would divide into two nines, calling themselves the Morning Glories and the Wide Awakes. Here they would play their games in the healthy hours of the morning, and then return home, dress in their citizens' clothes, eat their breakfasts and go to business.

This great enthusiasm in the game of baseball would hardly be indulged in at the present time, for who are there today who would arouse from their slumbers at the break of dawn and play a game of ball before the hours for business had arrived?

THE GREAT BASEBALL TOURNAMENT.

In September, 1867, commencing on Tuesday, the 24th, there was held here on the grounds of the Cincinnati Club, a grand baseball tournament, the like of which had never before been held, nor since, nor likely ever will be. A number of local and outside clubs participated, and the crowds gathered on those days were as large and as enthusiastic as any which are gathered to see a game of ball today. The attendance was immense. Crowds lined the fence. Hundreds of private vehicles were inside the grounds. Every available foot of ground was occupied, and more than five thousand ladies graced the occasion with their presence.

Prizes of much value were given, and the affair was a grand success in every way. The space of this book is such that we are unable to give a detailed account of all the games and the players, but we must mention the clubs that participated, and with whom they contested:

FIRST DAY.

Marions, 13; Ironside, 59.
Hickories, of McConnelsville, O., 41; Buckeyes, 25.
Scorers—James Sherwood and J. William Johnson.
Umpire—Dr. John Draper.

Base Ball in Cincinnati

SECOND DAY.

Great Westerns, 57; Gladiators, 22.
Socials, 14; Crescents, 41.
Copecs, of Covington, 16; Picked Nine, 26.
Eagles, of Dayton, Ky., 19; Indianolas, 52.

THIRD DAY.

Holts, of Newport, 55; Ironsides, 10.
Live Oaks, 64; Walnut Hills, 13.
Hickories, of McConnelsville, O., 16; Cincinnaiis, 28.

FOURTH DAY.

Crescents, 3; Reliables, of Covington, 38.
Live Oaks, 68; Great Westerns, 23.
Marions, 61; Crocketts, 30.
Baltics, 42; Osceolas, 33.
Scorers—M. Garrigan and M. O'Dowd.
Umpire—J.J. Sullivan.

FIFTH DAY.

Live Oaks, 30; Reliables, of Covington, 21.
Holts, of Newport, 26; Copecs, of Covington, 35.

THE PRIZE WINNERS.

Silver Ball.
First General Prize—Hickory Baseball Club, of McConnelsville, O.
Second General Prize—Live Oak Baseball Club, of Cincinnati.
Third General Prize—Copec Baseball Club, of Covington, Ky.
Fourth General Prize—Great Western Baseball Club, of Cincinnati.
Best Thrower to Bases—Lanfersieck, of the Live Oaks.
Farthest Throw—Charles H. Gould, of the Buckeyes. Distance, 302
feet and 3 inches.
Best Captain—Broackway, of the Live Oaks.

From an old drawing. Union Grounds, Cincinnati Baseball Club. Back of Lincoln Park, 1867–1871.

Swiftest Runner of Bases—Brookshaw, of the Buckeyes. Time, 15 3-4 seconds.

Best Catcher—Ryan, of the Holts, of Newport.

Best Pitcher—Bolan, of the Reliables, of Covington, Ky.

Best First Base—McConnell, of the Hickories, of McConnelsville, O.

Best Second Base—Charles H. Gould, of the Buckeyes.

Best Third Base—W.W. Pyle, of the Hickories, of McConnelsville, O.

Best Shortstop—John Howe, of the Holts, of Newport, Ky.

Best Left Field—Barnes, of the Copecs, of Covington, Ky.

Best Right Field—W. Boake, of the Buckeyes.
Best Center Field—Welsch, of the Reliables, of Covington.

The prizes were presented by George B. Ellard at his place of business on Main Street, where they had been placed on exhibition during the week.

The Cincinnati Club, being the host of the festivities, did not compete for any of the prizes.

Mr. Faulkner, then of the firm of Taylor & Faulkner, presented the Cincinnati Club with a very handsome silver service, which he awarded as a special prize. Mr. A.B. Champion, President of the Cincinnati Club, responded in a neat speech. He was followed by W.W. Ryan, President of the Hickory Baseball Club, and Judge Bellamy Storer, father of our former Minister to Austria.

FORMATION OF OHIO ASSOCIATION.

At the convention of the National Association of Baseball Players held December 12, 1866, it provided in its constitution for the formation and adoption of the various State associations.

For the purpose of forming an Ohio association, the presidents of the leading clubs in Cincinnati and the vicinity addressed circular letters to many of the clubs in a great number of the various towns and cities of Ohio, writing to each club to send delegates to assemble in Cincinnati upon September 26, 1867.

Forty-three clubs sent delegates, and they assembled in the large hall of the Clarendon Hotel. The meeting was called to order by Mr. A.B. Champion, who acted as temporary chairman, and George F. Sands as secretary. The Ohio Association was formed with the following officers:

A.B. Champion, President, of the Cincinnati Club.

W.W. Pyle, First Vice-President, of the Hickory Club, of McConnelsville.

W. A. McIntosh, Second Vice-President, of the Railway Union Club, of Cleveland.

Frank Harvey, Secretary, of the Buckeye Club.

J.T. Pringle, Corresponding Secretary, of the Republic Club, of Columbus.

Robert N. Spry, Treasurer, of the Riverside Club, Portsmouth.

The delegates from the local baseball clubs were:

Cincinnati—George B. Ellard and Aaron B. Champion.

Buckeye—George F. Sands and Frank Harvey.

From a recent photo. Dr. John Draper, *Organizer* Cincinnati Red Stocking Juniors, 1867.

Live Oak—John C. Davis and John Brockway.

Great Western—F.A. Taylor and William McKensie.

Crusaw—B.N. Parson and T. Norton.

Crescent—H.A. Deneke and Fred Pfister.

Columbia—Cyrus M. Potter and Albert Wratten.

Harmony—Adam A. Kramer and Lewis Straus.

Hun-ki-do-ri—T.J. McClure and D. Hauser.

I. X. L.—J. Knapp and J. Zimmerman.

Laurel—L. Rollwagen and N.C. Stoenle.

Marion—R.S. Crandell and J.M. White.

Pastime—H.D. Peck and E.D. Lovell.

Base Ball in Cincinnati

Red Hot—M.J. Higginson and J.H. St. Johns.
Social—E.D. Baker and C. Reckel.
East End—Sam Smiley and D. McClusker.
Fairmount—Fred Holmes and B.D. Jones.

SCORES MADE BY THE CINCINNATI BASEBALL CLUB DURING THE SEASON OF 1866.

			Red Stockings.	Opponents.	
September	29.	Buckeyes, of Cincinnati, O.	18	20	lost
October	18.	Buckeyes, of Cincinnati, O.	53	21	
"	26.	Copecs, of Covington, Ky.	27	21	
"	27.	Buckeyes, of Cincinnati, O.	31	41	lost

SCORES MADE BY THE CINCINNATI BASEBALL CLUB DURING THE SEASON OF 1867.

			Red Stockings.	Opponents.	
May	25.	Buckeyes, of Cincinnati, O.	53	40	
"	30.	Holts, of Newport, Ky.	82	33	
June	10.	Louisvilles, of Louisville, Ky.	42	19	
"	22.	Holts, of Newport, Ky.	93	22	
July	4.	Louisvilles, of Louisville, Ky.	60	24	
"	11.	Live Oaks, of Cincinnati, O.	56	18	
"	15.	Nationals, of Washington, D.C.	10	53	lost
August	9.	Live Oaks, of Cincinnati, O.	51	21	
"	29.	Great Westerns, of Cincinnati, O.	34	27	
September	2.	Holts, of Newport, Ky.	109	15	
"	6.	Louisvilles, of Louisville, Ky.	44	22	
"	7.	Olympics, of Washington, D.C.	77	17	
"	14.	Buckeyes, of Cincinnati, O.	28	20	
"	26.	Hickories, of McConnelsville, O.	28	16	
October	5.	Buckeyes, of Cincinnati, O.	49	23	
"	12.	Great Westerns, of Cincinnati, O.	17	15	
"	19.	Buckeyes, of Cincinnati, O.	37	23	
"	25.	Actives, of Indianapolis, Ind.	44	24	

In the game played on September 2 with the Holts, of Newport, Ky., the Cincinnati Club made thirty-one home runs.

So scarce were machine-made baseballs in Cincinnati during the early days of the game that some of the first balls ever sold by George B. Ellard, who then had the only baseball establishment in this city, were made by hand by Misses Margaret and Mary Truman, whose father was once a partner in the large book firm of Truman & Spofford, well remembered by our older citizens.

From a recent photo. James W. McLaughlin Designed the plans for the first Grand Stand, Cincinnati Baseball Club, 1867.

These young ladies held a high position in the exclusive social ranks in our city, but owing to financial reverses were thrown upon their own resources for a livelihood. Miss Mary Truman afterwards married Asa Brainard, the great pitcher of the Red Stockings of 1869.

CHAPTER III

*How the Famous Cincinnati Reds of 1868 Were Organized—Adop-
tion of the First Uniforms of the Club—Scores of 1868.*

The record of the Cincinnati Baseball Club in the years of the
latter '60s is one in which the citizens of Cincinnati take a local
pride. The story of the old club is rehearsed time and again by their
children and grandchildren in the present generation with the same
enthusiasm as that which animated the old players themselves.

With many, to be a son of the "Old Red Stockings" appears to
be as distinctive an honor as to be a Son of the Revolution or member of any other society of like character. Those members still living revive their memories and tell again the story of triumph with
reminiscent pleasure.

By the middle of 1867 the influence of baseball was being very
keenly felt in every direction, and new clubs were forming all around
the vicinity of the city. Newport, Covington and Dayton, Ky., had
their nines, while many of the suburbs were proud possessors of local
clubs; namely, Avondale, Walnut Hills, Clifton, Riverside and Mt.
Auburn. The fever had caught the younger element very strongly.

Dr. John Draper, afterwards clerk in the Police Department,
was the captain and catcher of the first game of baseball ever played
west of Pittsburg, when with the Live Oaks, in 1860. He umpired
the first game of baseball in Cincinnati, and during the years 1866

to 1870 umpired more match games of ball than any man in the West. He was one of the first delegates from Cincinnati to the National Association of Baseball Players at the annual convention held in New York at Clinton Hall, December 12, 1866, when he represented the Live Oaks, and was the first man from Ohio and the Central States to be appointed on a national committee—the Committee on Rules. He resigned from the Live Oak Baseball Club in 1867 and joined the Cincinnati Club. The Live Oak Club then played on the grounds of the Cincinnati Club.

Formation of the Cincinnati Junior Nines.

THE YOUNGSTERS OF THOSE DAYS WERE AS ACTIVE AND ENTHUSIASTIC AS THE LADS OF THE PRESENT TIME.

It was the latter part of 1867 that Dr. John Draper organized what was then known as the Cincinnati Juniors. These were all boys ranging in age from fifteen to twenty, and who wore the same uniform as the Cincinnati Baseball Club, and played frequently upon the latter's grounds.

The Junior Club included about twenty-five or thirty boys, who had divided themselves into two nines. One was composed of the older lads and the other of the younger. Among the players of the Juniors were to be found:

William H. Stewart, John V. Ellard, Charles Dean, Oscar Rammelsberg, Dr. E.W. Walker, George Chenowith, George A. Wiltsee, William Jones, Ad. R. Roll, S. Slocum, James Gladden, Pierce Butler, Oak Taylor, Joseph L. Marty, Frank Roth, Julius Hargrave, John Griffith, Charles A. Marsh, Edward Bradford, Smiley Walker,

From a recent photo. John V. Ellard, *Captain and Center Field* **Cincinnati Junior Baseball Team, 1868–1870.**

George "Scoop" Draper, Miller Outcalt, Edward H. Marsh, Ollie McGrew, Peregren "Pergy" Snodgrass, Harry Colbern, Albert Daggett, John Cameron, Charles Davis, Geo. W. Potter, Everett W. Hall, George Prather and James Maley.

The older nine of the Cincinnati Juniors was made up of the following players:

Harry Colbern	Catcher
Frank Roth	Pitcher
William Cottle	Shortstop
George Chenowith	First Base
Joseph L. Marty	Second Base
William Jones	Third Base
William H. Stewart	Right Field
John V. Ellard	Center Field and Captain
Oscar Rammelsberg	Left Field

William H. Stewart was the secretary of the nine, and John V. Ellard was the captain. The above was the regular nine, but when any were absent some of the other boys would take their places. Among them were Julius Hargrave, Edward Bradford, Geo. A. Wiltsee and Peregren Snodgrass, all of whom were excellent players. Joseph Marty acted as captain at one time.

The younger nine of the Cincinnati Juniors played continuously for three years without a change among their players, and scored over seventy-five games. It was composed of the following players:

Southey Holmes .... Catcher
James Shannon .... First Base
George W. Draper .... Shortstop
Edward Dunlap .... Pitcher and Captain
Miller Outcalt .... Second Base
Frank Dunlap .... Third Base
Joe Blair .... Left Field
Edward H. Marsh .... Center Field
Ollie McGrew .... Right Field

George Draper was given the familiar name of "Scoop," from the manner in which he fielded a ball. In fielding the ball he would always push his hands forward in a scooping manner to meet it.

These boys played together for three years with wonderful success, challenging every club of youngsters around. In the year 1869 they played all the clubs of boys within Hamilton County, O., and Kenton and Campbell Counties, in Kentucky, and never lost a game.

Miller Outcalt played as pretty a game at second base as McPhee ever did. George Draper was so good at shortstop that at nineteen years of age he was offered a fine salary by the management of one of the strongest clubs in the country to go with it and act in that capacity, but his brother, Dr. Draper, would not consent to have him go. Southey Holmes was a fine catcher, and could get as close to the bat and throw a ball as quickly and as correctly as any of them. Edward H. Marsh, as center fielder, was an excellent player.

Of this Junior nine, but four are living as we go to print. They are Joseph Blair, the Hamilton County recorder; Edward H. Marsh, a wealthy capitalist of Sandusky; Miller Outcalt, our prominent and efficient attorney, and Ollie McGrew. This Cincinnati Junior nine also played others outside of the State, as junior nines were being formed in all parts of the country.

There was also a junior nine among the Buckeye Baseball Club which had some very good players among the boys. They adopted the same uniform as the Buckeye Club, which was the same as the Cincinnati Club; namely, white flannel suits and red stockings, but instead of the letter C on their shirts they had the letter B.

Just as soon as the red stockings came into use by the Cincinnati Club, it seemed that every club that was formed here at that time adopted them.

The Buckeye Juniors were frequently matched against the Cincinnati Juniors, but most of the time the latter were just a little too strong for the former.

BUCKEYE JUNIORS.

Charles C. McBrair	Right Field
____ House	Catcher
____ Neiman	Pitcher
____ Trahy	Shortstop
Charles Ulmer	First Base
____ Dickman	Second Base
____ O'Dowd	Third Base
Harry Crane	Left Field
____ Sunman	Center Field

There were also other nines of youngsters located in our different suburbs during the latter sixties. Prominent among them was the Pickwick Baseball Club, of Walnut Hills. This club was organized in the fall of 1867, and had the reputation of defeating every nine of boys with whom they contested, with the exception of the Cincinnati Juniors, for these boys never made a match with the Pickwicks. This club existed from 1867 to 1872, when, at that time, many of the boys were obliged to go to the Eastern colleges, thus breaking up the club. Chas. A. Gould was the secretary of the club.

Standing—Frank Dunlap, 3rd B.; Joe Blair, L. F.; Edward H. Marsh, C. F.; Miller Outcalt, 2nd B. Sitting—George Draper, S. S.; Ollie McGrew, R. F.; Ed Dunlap, P.; Southey Holmes, C.; Jas. Shannon, 1st B. Cincinnati Junior Baseball Team of 1868. From an original photo taken at the time.

One of the most interesting games played by the Pickwicks was in the spring of 1868, when they were matched with the first nine of the Fairmount Baseball Club, of Fairmount. The score in the ninth inning stood 35 to 35, and when the tenth inning started great enthusiasm was displayed on both sides, but the Pickwicks came out victorious in a score of 51 to 36. We give below the players on each side, with the score made on that day:

PICKWICKS.

Preach Marsh .... Pitcher

Thomas Wheelright .... Right Field
Thomas Macavoy .... Center Field
Charles A. Gould .... Second Base
Willis Kemper .... First Base
Nap Trenner .... Left Field
Harry Hattersley .... Catcher
Chas. Van .... Shortstop
Dick George .... Third Base

FAIRMOUNTS.

Golden .... Pitcher
Richards .... Right Field
Merryweather .... Center Field
Chandler .... Second Base
Moor .... First Base
Taggert .... Left Field
Beasley .... Catcher
Stewart .... Shortstop
Minor .... Third Base

The game lasted 2 hours and 40 minutes. Douglas Allison, of the Cincinnati Club, was the umpire, and Messrs. Francisco and Lang were the scorers.

Innings	1	2	3	4	5	6	7	8	9	10
Pickwicks	0	14	5	2	2	1	5	2	4	16—51
Fairmounts	0	8	6	0	0	10	1	2	8	1—36

Joe Griffith and William Seeds were also good players of the Pickwick Club. The regular grounds of the club were called the River Hill Grounds, and were located where the residences of Mr. Thomas P. Egan, Mr. Lawrence Maxwell and Judge Howard Ferris now stand.

From a recent photo. Hon. William H. Taft, *Member*. Mt. Auburn Baseball Club, 1868.

Mount Auburn fell into line with her nine of boys, which was composed of a lot of youngsters whose enthusiasm in the game was as unbounded as that of the members of the senior organizations. Their grounds were located on the present site of the Riding Club, and near where the catcher stood was a pond where the boys would alternate swimming with a game of baseball. The ball would frequently fall into the pond, and Mel Strobridge, the catcher, would often practice a great fishing feat in reaching after it with a long pole. The first bat used by the boys was of home manufacture, having been made out of an old wagon shaft procured from the neighboring blacksmith shop. It was a good one, nevertheless, for it lasted a long while. The boys wore the same uniform as the Cincinnati Baseball Club. The team of the Mount Auburn Baseball Club was:

Cliff Williams .... Pitcher
J. Melvin Strobridge .... Catcher
Oliver Kinsey .... Shortstop
Albert Whetstone .... Center Field
Nelson Perry .... Second Base
George Kolker .... Third Base
Rufus B. Smith .... Right Field

Base Ball in Cincinnati

Charles L. Burgoyne .... Left Field
William M. Allen .... First Base and Captain

There were some other good players connected with the Mount Auburn Baseball Club, including William H. Taft, our Secretary of War; Stewart Shillito, C.A. Bennett, R. Douglas, S. Douglas and Thomas Allen.

The Avondale youngsters were so enthusiastic over the game of baseball that enough were gathered together in that village to form two nines. One was made up of the younger element and one of the older. Their grounds were located about where the new Jewish Temple now stands, and many were the exciting games played there.

Lewis W. Irwin was the captain of the older nine, and was considered the heaviest batter among the boys at that time. He could use either his left or right hand with equal dexterity, and in this way he puzzled the pitcher of the contesting nine to such an extent, and batted the ball with such force, that a home run was often placed to his credit. John C. Hart was also an excellent player.

The older nine of the Avondale boys had for their players:

J. Wayne Neff .... Pitcher
William Greenwood .... Catcher
John C. Hart .... Shortstop
Dan O'Connell .... First Base
James Campbell .... Second Base
Lewis W. Irwin .... Third Base and Captain
Samuel Hart .... Right Field
George Cloon .... Center Field
Jordon P. Hart .... Left Field

The younger nine of Avondale boys had for their players:

Charley Dury .... Pitcher and Captain
Henry Dury .... Catcher
Frank Phipps .... Shortstop
William Woodward .... First Base
Charles Evans .... Second Base
George Peachey .... Third Base
George Haven .... Left Field
George Winston .... Right Field
W.O. Coffin .... Center Field

Clifton was not all behind with her young nine of baseball fans. They were all excellent and enthusiastic players, and the team was composed of the following boys:

William McAlpin .... Pitcher
John C. Sherlock .... Catcher
George Smith .... Shortstop
Wilson Smith .... First Base
Charles H. Resor .... Third Base
Edward Andrews .... Second Base and Captain
Albert Bennett .... Left Field
James Keyes .... Center Field
Charles Wells .... Right Field

The other members of the club were: John Brown, William Brotherton, H. Keyes, H. Von Phul, H. Hughes, Thomas Barclay.

The Clifton boys often played with the lads on the other hill-tops, and their scores were very creditable.

There was also a nine of boys on East Walnut Hills, who called themselves the Woodburn Baseball Club, and whose grounds were near the corner of Woodburn Avenue and Chapel Street. Many of the Junior nines from the other suburbs and from the city often came to these grounds to play the Woodburns. Among the players were: E.W. Walker, George H. Koker, Dick George, Salsbury French, Joseph Griffith, _____ Ralfey.

At the twelfth convention of the National Association of Baseball Players, held in Philadelphia, December 11 and 12, 1867, the junior clubs of the country were represented by delegates. In looking over the minutes of the two days' session, we find a reference to them in the following words: "The great majority of delegates present were gentlemen of character and influence, who would have reflected credit on any legislative assemblage of the kind in the country."

The Ohio Federation of the National Association was organized September 25, 1867, with Aaron B. Champion, President, and Frank Harvey, Secretary, and the delegates to the convention that year were George F. Sands and J.A. Scarrit, who represented forty-two clubs in Ohio, fourteen of which were in Cincinnati.

During the winter of 1867-'68 the grounds of the Cincinnati Baseball Club were flooded for skating purposes, and it was here that the first game of baseball was played on skates. The interest in baseball was so great then that even the winter did not lessen the enthusiasm in the game.

Edward H. Marsh, *Center Fielder* **Cincinnati Junior Baseball Team, 1868.**

Chapter III

MEN ON THE TEAM.

In the latter part of 1867 the Cincinnati Club formed a regularly organized nine to play throughout the coming year, and it was known as the first nine. This was composed of the following players:

Harry Wright	Pitcher
Fred Waterman	Third Base
Douglas Allison	Catcher
Charles H. Gould	First Base
Asa Brainard	Second Base
J. William Johnson	Right Field
Rufus King	Center Field
J.V.B. Hatfield	Left Field
John Con How	Shortstop
Moses Grant	Substitute

The above were the regular positions of the players, but occasionally they would change about a little.

The origin of the uniform of the Cincinnati Baseball Club is not generally known. When baseball first started, the players adopted a uniform similar to that used by the cricket clubs—shirt, cap and long trousers. At a meeting held in the office of Aaron B. Champion, then at 75 West Third Street, the subject of uniform was discussed and a number of designs were submitted. That designed and submitted by George B. Ellard, namely, short white flannel trousers, white flannel shirt and red stockings, was finally accepted and adopted, hence the origin of the name of the club. As the long red stockings were necessarily made to order, they were quite expensive, for they were up to that time unknown.

Woman Made First Uniforms.

The orders for the manufacture of the uniforms for the nines of 1867-'68-'69-'70 were given by Mr. Ellard to Mrs. Bertha Bertram, who at that time conducted a tailoring establishment on Elm Street, near Elder. Mrs. Bertram has the distinction of making the first uniforms that were ever worn by members of the Cincinnati Baseball Club, the style of which has been changed but very little up to the present day. She also made the uniforms for other clubs which came into existence here during the seventies and early eighties, among which were the Ravens, Shamrocks, Stars, Riversides, Mutuals (of Cumminsville), and many others.

It will be interesting to note just at this point the style of the uniforms used by other clubs in the country; one in particular which we have in mind is that of the Louisville Baseball Club, of Louisville, Ky. This club was organized April 10, 1865, and the uniform which they adopted and used for some time, consisted of a grey flannel shirt, trimmed with scarlet; black and white check cap, blue jeans pants and black patent leather belt.

A Great Base Runner.

In 1868 the New York *Clipper* offered nine very handsome gold medals, to be given among those players of all clubs in the country who made the best averages in their respective positions. The Cincinnati Club captured three of them, being awarded to J. Hatfield, as left fielder; Fred Waterman, as third baseman, and J. William Johnson, the well-known and popular attorney of our city, as right fielder. Mr. Johnson was considered the swiftest runner on the bases in his day, and held the record of running around the four bases in fourteen and a half seconds. Mr. Berthong, the catcher and right fielder of the Nationals, was the only one in the country to excel Mr. Johnson's time, his being just the fraction of a second under Mr. Johnson's. One would hardly believe today, when looking at the little, good-natured, gray-haired lawyer, as he sits at his desk in the Fourth National Bank Building, that he held the enviable record of never having been put out while stealing a base, and on several occasions succeeded in stealing home from third. He could fill the position of second or third base, as well as right field, with equal dexterity and success.

A WONDERFUL BALL THROWER.

J.V.B. Hatfield, the great left fielder and catcher of the Cincinnati Club, was a wonderful thrower. One day upon the grounds he threw a baseball over the field six times, three times with the wind and three times against, covering the distances respectively of 123, 129 and 132 yards, and 127, 127, and 126 yards. The judges of the throws were "Doc" John Draper, at the point of throwing, and J.C. How and Harry Wright, where the ball dropped. The measurements were taken by Harry Wright and George B. Ellard. Others afterwards took the measurements to verify those taken officially by Wright and Ellard.

This record stood for some time, but in October of 1872, upon the Union Grounds in Brooklyn, Hatfield threw the ball a distance of 133 yards, 1 foot and 7½ inches.

In September and October of 1888, there was a contest given in Cincinnati, under the auspices of the Cincinnati *Enquirer*, when Ed. W. Williamson threw a ball the distance of 133 yards and 11

From a recent photo. J. William Johnson, *Right Fielder* Cincinnati Baseball Team, 1868.

inches, just 8½ inches under that made by Hatfield.

The games of 1868 were exceedingly interesting, and one especially is called to mind, played August 26, with the Unions, of Morrisania, N.Y. The wildest enthusiasm prevailed among the spectators at this game, the innings being so close that it was difficult to foresee who would win. The game finally ended with a score of 13 to 12, in the Reds' favor. The excitement of the ladies present reached its highest pitch, hand-kerchiefs were waved, and cheer upon cheer from the fair sex went forth as each inning was decided. One enthusiastic woman present waved her parasol high in the air, and, not noticing the close prox-imity of a gentleman's head in front of her, brought it down with such force upon his cranium that the handle broke, leaving her parasol a wreck and tears of pain welling up in the eyes of her victim. "Oh, pardon me," she cried, in dismay. "Do not mention it," he replied, with gallantry; "I suffer for a good cause." The men recklessly threw their hats in the field, to see them trodden under foot, with not a sign of regret. It was esti-mated that there were 10,000 people present, one-half of whom were ladies, the wives, mothers, sisters and sweethearts of the boys all wanting the Reds to win, as all felt a self-interest in the game. It was not an uncommon occurrence to see a hundred or more private carriages present on the grounds at these early games. The club that year was occupying grounds just back of Lincoln Park, having moved from its previous ones at the foot of Richmond Street the latter part of 1867, as these new grounds were more convenient to the horse cars, which then ran in front of the park, in Freeman Street. These grounds were leased at an annual rental of $2,000.

GROWTH OF THE SPORT.

The interest in the various games had increased to such an extent that the attendance was becoming larger at each game played. It was found necessary to increase the seating capacity, and plans were submitted to erect a large octagonal building at the southeast corner of the grounds. Those designed by James McLaughlin, the architect, were accepted, and the building was erected at a cost of $2,350.

As the Cincinnati Club did not require its grounds every day in the week, upon those days when they were not used the privilege of playing on the grounds was rented out to various other local clubs at a rental of $25 per month.

The clubs that used them were the Live Oaks, the Charter Oak, the Great Western and the Buckeye. When any local club had a game with the Cincinnati Club on its grounds they were given one-third of the net receipts, and when an Eastern or outside club came to play they were allowed one-half of the net receipts.

Another game which is called to mind was played August 5, 1868, with the Hickory Baseball Club, of McConnelsville, O. This club was the pride of Morgan County, and it was considered by its admirers, no less than in its own estimation, the toughest timber that ever stepped over the grassy field. The game was played here, and just before it was called the catcher of the Hickorys, whose height was about six feet four, and whose hair was as fine a carrot color as any one wished to see, asked for the information that should he knock a ball over the fence would he be allowed a home run.

He was answered in the affirmative, when a broad grin spread over his face, which said as much, "What easy marks we have run against." When the game ended it was plainly noticeable that this tall herculean wonder never scored a run, having struck out the first two times he went to the bat. The pitcher of that famous nine was also a very bright individual. When a man was stealing second from first, while the ball was in his hands, he would throw it to second backwards without looking around; it invariably went wide of its mark and runners reached second safely. The game resulted in a score of 59 to 16 in favor of the Reds. The bat used in these early games was about the same as it is now and the ball was a trifle larger, but it contained two and one-half ounces of rubber, and it was probably owing to this cause that the scores were larger than those made today. The diamond was the same size, but the field was of greater dimensions. The standard ball of '68 was made by a man named

The New York Clipper Medal. *Won by J. William Johnson.* **Being judged the best player in his position among all of the clubs in the country in 1868.**

Ross, whose establishment was in Brooklyn, N.Y. They were all hand-made, and cost $2.50 each, while a good bat would cost $1.50.

Not only did the game of baseball inspire the Cincinnati Club to achieve the most wonderful scores in the game, but it stimulated the poetic muse to give expression to verses of more than ordinary merit. Many, many years before "Casey at the Bat" had ever appeared, the divine afflatus welled up in the brain of a member of the Cincinnati Baseball Club in the latter sixties, and the following poem appeared in many of the papers of the time, showing the high esteem in which the players whose names are mentioned were held:

The Cincinnati Baseball Club Song.

BY A MEMBER.
(AIR— *"Bonnie Blue Flag."*)

We are a band of baseball players
    From "Cincinnati City;"
We come to toss the ball around,
    And sing to you our ditty.
And if you listen to our song
    We are about to sing,
We'll tell you all about baseball,
    And make the welkin ring.
        CHORUS.

Hurrah! Hurrah!
    For the noble game, hurrah!
"Red Stockings" all will toss the ball,
    And shout our loud hurrah.

Our Captain is a goodly man,
    And Harry is his name;

Base Ball in Cincinnati

Whate'er he does, 'tis always "Wright,"
  So says the voice of fame.
And as the Pitcher of our nine,
  We think he can't be beat;
In many a fight, old Harry Wright
  Has saved us from defeat.
            CHORUS.

The man who catches Harry's balls,
  It passes all belief,
He's so expert in catching "fouls,"
  We have dubbed him "chicken thief."
And if a player's on his first,
  He'd better hold it fast;
With "Johnny Hat" behind the bat,
  The balls are seldom passed.
            CHORUS.

In many a game that we have played,
  We've needed a First Base,
But now our opponents will find
  The "basket" in its place.
And if you think he "muffs" the balls,
  Sent into him red hot,
You'll soon be fooled by "Charlie Gould,"
  And find he "muffs" them not.
            CHORUS.

We travel on to Second Base,
  And Brainard there is found;
He beats the world in catching "flies,"
  And covering the ground.
And as the Pitcher of our nine,
  Whene'er 'tis best to change,

The man will find that plays behind,
  That "Asa" has the range.
            CHORUS.

And lest the boys should thirsty get
  When after balls they've ran,
We take with us, where'er we go,
  A jolly "Waterman."
Upon Third Base he stops hot balls,
  And sends them in so fine,
That all have said that jolly "Fred"
  Is home upon the nine.
            CHORUS.

Our Shortstop is a man of worth,
  We hope he'll never die;
He stops all balls that come to him;
  He's grim death on the "fly."
The many deeds he has performed,
  We will not here relate,
But tell you now that "Johnny How"
  As a player is first-rate.
            CHORUS.

The infield now is traveled o'er;
  The out comes next in line,
And "Moses Grant" is brought to view,
  Right Fielder in our nine.
He knows the place, he plays right well,
  To none the palm he'll yield;
He's bound you shan't catch "Moses Grant"
  A "napping" in right field.
            CHORUS.

There is a man upon our nine,
  To him a verse we'll sing;

You all have heard of him before,
  His name is Rufus King.
Just now he plays as Center Field,
  Sometimes as Second Base;
We all have proof that merry "Ruf"
  Is worthy of the place.
          CHORUS.

Come, fill your glasses to the brim
  With joyous, sparkling wine,
And drink a toast to all that's "Left"
  Of the 'riginal First Nine.
Of all the men who first essayed
  Upon that nine to play,
There's only one, and that's "Johnson,"
  Who holds a place today.
          CHORUS.

To win the game we play today,
  We earnestly shall try,
And hope our expectations won't
  Be captured on the "fly."
We shall expect a quick return
  To toss the ball around;
We'll welcome all to games of ball
  Upon our "Union Ground."
          CHORUS.

HARRY WRIGHT MARRIED.

The date of September 10, 1868, marked the marriage of Harry Wright, the hero and idol of the Cincinnati Baseball Club. The evening of his marriage the club presented him with a handsome gold watch, with a $100 five per cent. Government bond in which the watch was wrapped, as an appreciation of the kindly feeling it had for him, and for the faithful and efficient work he had done on the field. The members of the nine of the Cincinnati Club also presented Mr. Wright with a beautiful gold medal, upon which was inscribed his name with those of all the players on the nine.

BASEBALL CORRESPONDENTS AND SPORTING EDITORS.

From a recent photo. Joseph Blair, *Left Fielder* Cincinnati Junior Baseball Team, 1868.

It seemed that especial care was taken to make the reports of these games of early days very interesting.

The sporting editors and correspondents of the various journals throughout the country sent in the most reliable and impartial information. Even their own personal enthusiasm never allowed their judgment to go astray, and very few instances occurred where any of their statements were called into question. So much was thought of the efforts of these gentlemen that at one of the conventions held by the National Association of Baseball Players they passed the following flattering tribute upon

Standing—Asa Brainard, P. and 2nd B.; J. William Johnson, R. F. and
L. F.; J.V.B. Hatfield, C. and L. F.; Rufus King, C. F.; John C. Howe,
S. S. Sitting—Harry Wright, P.; Fred Waterman, 3rd B.; Chas. H.
Gould, 1st B.; Moses Grant, R.F. Cincinnati Baseball Team of 1868.
From an original photo taken by Van Loo on the grounds at the time.

Mr. Henry Chadwick, who was connected with the New York *Clipper*:

"We deem it proper to pay a tribute to our friend, Mr. Henry
Chadwick, a gentleman who has had long experience in the report-
ing of baseball, cricket and aquatics for several journals, and whose
reports are universally admitted to be of a reliable, impartial and tal-
ented character. Mr. Chadwick bestows a care, attention and pains
upon his reports which have won for them a standard reputation and
influence with all who take any interest in American outdoor pas-
times. Knowing and appreciating their worth and value, it affords us

sincere pleasure and gratification to add our humble testimony in behalf of their conceded merit and excellence."

INDIANS PLAY ON THE UNION GROUNDS.

During the summer of 1868 the Cincinnati Baseball Club presented a novel attraction for the citizens. They brought a number of Indians from the Northwest to play a game of raquette on their grounds. This was a game among the Indians similar to that of la crosse. In their gay attire and painted faces they presented a very picturesque appearance and afforded much enjoyment to the spectators, as this was the first time anything of the kind ever appeared in Cincinnati. They were given the clubhouse in which to camp during their visit, and it is well remembered that it took a month to deodorize the premises which they had occupied.

There were also some exciting and amusing games played in 1868 which were not down on the regular schedule for the Union Grounds. One of these was played on July 12 between the Book Shovers, or Robert Clarke & Company, and the Eclectics, of Wilson, Hinkle & Company, which is now the American Book Company. The Book Shovers' nine was composed of the following players:

Edward Woodruff .... Pitcher
Harvey Anderson .... Shortstop
____ McClintock .... Catcher
____ Ayres .... First Base
John Dickinson .... Second Base
Walter Wild .... Third Base
Charles Wild .... Left Field
R.D. Barney .... Center Field
____ Stoerle .... Right Field

The Eclectics had the following players on their nine:

A. Howard Hinkle .... Pitcher and Captain
George Werner .... Catcher
_____ Tinsley .... Shortstop
George Beggs .... First Base
Samuel Dustin .... Second Base
Henry C. Sherick .... Third Base
Harry T. Ambrose .... Left Field
James McCormick .... Center Field
Robert F. Leaman .... Right Field
Louis Gerling .... Change Pitcher
W. B. Thalheimer .... Scorer

The Eclectics worked hard to win the game, but they were finally obliged to give way to the Book Shovers in a score of 46 to 28.

Woman Reports Game.

Another game was played on October 8 of the same year, which was quite an event among the social circles of our city. There were a great many ladies present, and this is the first game of baseball in Cincinnati that was reported to the papers by a woman. The contesting teams were the Biscuits and the Muffins.

The Biscuits.

Major J.J. McDowell .... Catcher
Hunter Brooke .... Pitcher
F. Armstrong .... First Base
W.S. Ridgway .... Second Base
Major Newlin .... Third Base
A.H. Bugher .... Shortstop

Nathaniel Wright .... Left Field
Major Norton .... Center Field
Joseph How .... Right Field

THE MUFFINS.

John Burnet .... Catcher
T.H. Wright .... Pitcher
T. Taylor .... First Base
_____ Atkinson .... Second Base
Major Howell .... Third Base
William Williamson .... Shortstop
Captain McIntosh .... Left Field
W. Shoenberger .... Center Field
Major Lowe .... Right Field

The ladies were vociferous in their cheers, and waved their parasols and handkerchiefs at every good move made on the part of the players. Major McDowell made five home runs on that day, but was put out—of breath—several times. Nat Wright fielded well, and caught many high flies as well as the frequent smiles of the ladies. Billy Williamson also caught many side glances from the fair sex. The game ended in a score of 41 to 34 in favor of the Biscuits. A number of officers from the Newport Barracks were present to witness this game.

From his last photo taken 1904. Major J.J. McDowell, *Member* **Cincinnati Baseball Club, 1866–1871.**

Sedate and staid old Third Street also got into line with its baseball teams. Bankers and insurance men came down off of their high pedestals and joined in the furor of the day. An interesting game was played between the members of the First National Bank and those of the Third National. One can scarcely imagine, to look at these staid and elderly gentlemen living today, that they ever took part in a game of baseball, but they still recall the fact with pleasure and dwell upon it as a happy reminiscence. We give the players on both sides. The game was played in July, 1868.

FIRST NATIONALS.

Harry Guild .... First Base
Charles Phaler .... Catcher
Dick Williamson .... Second Base
R. Purcell .... Center Field
Samuel McKeehan .... Third Base
G.W. Forbes .... Pitcher
Frank Guild .... Right Field
Allen Hinchman .... Shortstop
C.F. Tower .... Left Field

THIRD NATIONALS.

H.C. Yergason .... Pitcher
John Findlay .... Left Field
Charles Nash .... Catcher
W.P. Thomas .... Center Field
Samuel W. Ramp .... Shortstop
George McLaughlin .... Third Base
W.S. Griffith .... First Base
William Worthington .... Second Base
Griffith P. Griffith .... Right Field

Fred Waterman, of the Cincinnati Club, umpired the game,

which resulted in a score of 36 to 21 in favor of the Third Nationals.

The insurance men of Third Street were not to be outdone when it came to a game of baseball, so they challenged the Bankers to a game, which drew a large attendance and great enthusiasm.

THE INSURANCE NINE.

H.A. Glassford .... Pitcher
Charles S. Scanlan .... Catcher
C. McCord .... First Base
E.E.Townley .... Second Base
J.H. Beattie .... Third Base
H. Van Valkenberg .... Shortstop
S.B. Markland .... Right Field
B.F. Davidson .... Center Field
S.C. Benjamin .... Left Field

THE BANKERS.

Charles Nash .... Pitcher
S. Ramp .... Catcher
G.W. Forbes .... First Base
Thomas Johnson .... Second Base
"Tave" Tudor .... Third Base
H.C. Yergason .... Shortstop
R.W. Richey .... Right Field
M.V.B. Lee .... Center Field

The game ended in a score of 43 to 25 in favor of the Bankers. Home runs were made by Yergason, Markland, Glassford, Tudor, Lee, Johnson, Ramp and Forbes. This great game was played on the 1st of August, 1868.

Cincinnati possessed a number of baseball clubs during the year 1868 which frequently played matches on the grounds of the Cincinnati Club, and drew a large attendance at each of the games played. They were—

Crescent Baseball Club.
Avenue Baseball Club.
Columbia Baseball Club, of Columbia.
East End Baseball Club.
Fairmount Baseball Club.
Ironsides Baseball Club.
I. X. L. Baseball Club.
Pastime Baseball Club.
Red Hook Baseball Club.
Walnut Hills Baseball Club.
Lightfoot Baseball Club, of
    Madisonville.
Crusaw Baseball Club, of
    Pendleton.
Harmony Baseball Club.
Hun-ki-do-ri Baseball Club.
Laurel Baseball Club.
Marion Baseball Club.
Red Hot Baseball Club.
Social Baseball Club.
Independent Baseball Club.
Banner Baseball Club.
Osceola Baseball Club.
Baltic Baseball Club.
Indianola Baseball Club.
Reliable Baseball Club, of Covington, Ky.
Crockett Baseball Club.

From his last photo taken 1907.
Col. Thomas F. Shay, *Catcher*
Baltic Baseball Team, 1868.

Chapter III

Eagle Baseball Club, of Dayton, Ky.
Monitor Baseball Club.
Ludlow Baseball Club, of Ludlow, Ky.
Arctic Baseball Club.
Resolute Baseball Club.
Irving Baseball Club, of Covington, Ky.
Haymaker Baseball Club, of Covington, Ky.
Alaska Baseball Club.

SCORES MADE BY THE CINCINNATI BASEBALL CLUB
DURING THE SEASON OF 1868.

			Red Stockings.	Opponents.	
May	6.	Great Westerns, of Cincinnati	41	7	
	9.	Xenias, of Xenia, O.	51	19	
	21.	Copecs, of Covington, Ky.	30	14	
	23.	Buckeyes, of Cincinnati	28	10	
	30.	Live Oaks, of Cincinnati	72	5	
June	6.	Athletics, of Philadelphia, Pa.	13	20	lost
	11.	Riversides, of Portsmouth, O.	59	17	
	20.	Miamis, of Yellow Springs, O.	71	12	
	27.	Xenias, of Xenia, O.	60	13	
July	2.	Railway Unions, of Cleveland, O.	52	16	
	4.	Unions, of St. Louis, Mo.	70	7	
	6.	Athletics, of Philadelphia, Pa.	19	40	lost
	13.	Copecs, of Covington, Ky.	53	4	
	24.	Riversides, of Portsmouth, O.	34	16	
	27.	Live Oaks, of Cincinnati	53	11	
	29.	Live Oaks, of Cincinnati	48	3	
Aug.	3.	Railway Unions, of Columbus, O.	34	16	
	4.	Capitols, of Columbus, O.	43	5	
	5.	Hickories, of McConnelsville, O.	59	16	
	6.	Baltics, of Wheeling, W. Va.	66	8	
	7.	Mears, of Steubenville, O.	60	20	
	8.	Olympics, of Pittsburg, Pa.	29	14	
	10.	Alleghenies, of Allegheny City, Pa.	25	13	
	12.	Forest Citys, of Cleveland, O.	44	22	
	24.	Unions, of Morrisania, N.Y.	8	12	lost

			Red Stockings.	Opponents.	
	25.	Unions, of Morrisania, N.Y.	13	12	
	29.	Buckeyes, of Cincinnati	20	12	
Sept.	14.	Actives, of Indianapolis, Ind.	54	7	
	16.	Live Oaks, of Cincinnati	38	17	
	17.	Great Westerns, of Cincinnati	38	2	
	19.	Excelsiors, of Rochester, N.Y.	27	11	
	20.	Excelsiors, of Rochester, N.Y.	22	4	
	23.	Nationals, of Washington, D.C.	16	10	
	24.	Olympics, of Washington, D.C.	9	22	lost
	25.	Enterprises, of Baltimore, Md.	24	3	
	27.	Athletics, of Philadelphia, Pa.	12	15	lost
	28.	Olympics, of Philadelphia, Pa.	41	20	
Oct.	1.	Atlantics, of Brooklyn, N.Y.	12	31	lost
	2.	Mutuals, of New York City, N.Y.	29	28	
	3.	Unions, of Morrisania, N.Y.	Refused to play.		
	4.	Keystones, of Philadelphia, Pa.	22	24	lost
	6.	Unions of Haymakers, of Lansingburg, N.Y.	27	8	
	7.	Excelsiors, of Rochester, N.Y.	21	11	
	8.	Niagaras, of Buffalo, N.Y.	24	8	
	9.	Nationals, of Albany, N.Y.	17	1	
	11.	Railway Unions, of Cleveland, O.	41	8	
	12.	Forest Citys, of Cleveland, O.	33	14	
	17.	Picked Nine, of Cincinnati	32	15	
Nov.	2.	Picked Nine, of Cincinnati	38	21	

The Red Stockings had arranged some months before to play the Unions, of Morrisania, on October 3, while they were on their Eastern tour. This game was to have been played just after the Red Stockings had played their game with the Mutuals, of New York City.

The rule was, at this time, that if the champion club (which was the Union in 1867) had lost two games out of three with some other club, they were to resign their title to the winning club. The Unions had lost and won a game with the Red Stockings, and had also done the same thing with the Mutuals, of New York. When the

From a recent photo. Hon. Thomas J. Cogan, *Right Fielder* Baltic Baseball Team, 1868.

Cincinnati Club was to play the deciding game with the Unions, they were subjected to one of the meanest and most ungentlemanly tricks ever imposed upon a baseball club.

Early in the season the New York *Clipper* had offered a gold ball to the club which won the championship in 1868, and the Unions, fearing that the prize might be carried off by a Western club, instead of playing the Red Stockings, came to New York and played the Mutuals, with whom they lost the championship, thus making it impossible for the Cincinnati Club to have a chance to win the cherished trophy, as they had already played their game with the Mutuals. Other games were played in the East, the Athletics, of Philadelphia, finally winning the pennant. The New York *Clipper*, published in October of 1868, commented on this episode in the following:

"We wish to allude to the treatment of the Cincinnati Club, of Cincinnati, O., by the Unions, of Morrisania. On their Western tour the Unions won and lost a game with the Cincinnati Club. It was claimed by the Unions that the game lost was merely an exhibition game and did not count in the series. Our special correspondent, who accompanied the Unions, so recorded it, but we stated at the time, with appended note to his remarks, that we regarded it as a match game, and we have since understood that the Western champions so regarded it. On their recent Eastern tour, the Cincinnatis were advertised to play the Unions on the 3d inst., but upon the arrival of the visiting club in the metropolis, they heard that the Unions would not play them. * * * We do know that the Western players expected that the game would come off, and were considerably disappointed in the failure of the Unions to meet them."

A similar treatment was imposed upon the Atlantics, of Brooklyn, N.Y., by the Unions, as the Atlantics had challenged the Unions in the early part of the season to play matches for the championship.

When, on October 11th and 12th, the Cincinnati Club played their games with the Forest City and Railway Union Baseball Clubs, of Cleveland, Ohio, the Cleveland papers commented on the players of the Cincinnati nine. "Since it has come to be that a State or city is in so important a sense represented by its leading baseball clubs, it must have been a gratifying thing to the visitors at the ball grounds on Saturday to find that our State is represented abroad by a club so eminent in all the amenities of good behavior and gentlemanly deportment, as well as sharp, unerring play. A body of lithe, well-formed young men, with clear, intelligent, manly faces, quiet and reserved on the field, and of unexceptional morals, such is the Cincinnati Club, the darling and the pride of the city whose name it bears. Five hundred members, including many prominent gentlemen of the city, constitute its organization. Its games are watched and read over as the sensation of the hour, and the sturdiest voices

Opposite: **Diagram of a baseball field, 1868.**

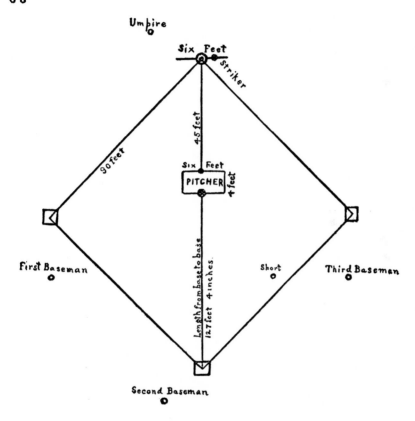

as well as the daintiest mouchoirs of Porkopolis are raised to celebrate its victories."

FORM OF APPLICATION FOR MEMBERSHIP
INTO THE CINCINNATI BASEBALL CLUB.

CINCINNATI, O...................

M.............................

I hereby authorize and request you to present my name as a Candidate for Membership to the

CINCINNATI BASEBALL CLUB,

of Cincinnati, Ohio, and pledge me, if elected, to the support of the Constitution and By-Laws of said Club.

I am not a member of, or indebted for any dues, fines or assessments to any Baseball Club belonging to the "National Association of Baseball Players," at the time of making this application.

Name, ...

Residence, ...

Place of Business, ...

Proposed by ....

Seconded by ....

The charter roll of membership of the Cincinnati Baseball Club, from the years 1866 to 1871, is in the possession of the writer. It is handsomely inscribed and decorated upon a large piece of parchment, and for a number of years hung on the club-room wall in a neat frame. The following is an exact copy of all the names enrolled thereon:

Chapter III

W.G. Allen.
W.L. Avery.
D.E. Adams.
G.W.P. Atkinson.
Larz Anderson.
Nicholas Longworth Anderson.
C.E. Anderson.
K.B. Ashfield.
L. Apjones.
A. Adae.
Matthew Addy.
Douglas Allison.
Asa Brainard.
A.P.C. Bonte.
C.E. Bonte.
C.M. Beesley.
Harry Beesley.
J.H. Bascom.
Silas Bascom.
George Bascom.
Julius Blackburn.
Howard B. Bates.
Harry C. Bates.
Isaac Bates, Jr.
N.P. Batlett.
R.M. Blatchford.
Hunter Brooke.
F.F. Brookes.
James H. Beattie.
Samuel J. Baker.
George W. Baker.

W.F. Burton.
R.B. Burton.
Ammi Baldwin.
W.H. Baldwin.
F.H. Baldwin.
William P. Babbitt.
W.J. Breed.
H.P. Belknap.
W.E. Brown.
H.N. Brown.
J.W. Batchelor.
A. Bevis.
J.F. Brewster.
W.C. Boothe.
A.D. Bullock.
James A. Bailey.
James R. Brockway.
C.A. Boynton.
Aaron B. Champion.
S.M. Chester.
William H. Calvert.
C. Calvert.
J.E. Cochnower.
W.H. Chatfield.
Theodore Cook.
M.H. Crane.
G.F. Cooke.
Quinton Corwine.
Robert W. Carroll.
William M. Caldwell.
Charles E. Callahan.

A.G. Corre.
Alf. Cutter.
Enoch T. Carson.
W.A. Clarke.
H. Colville.
E.W. Coles.
James Cunningham.
G.G. Cox.
A.J. Clark.
Charles Coleman.
Edward T. Comergys.
William B. Carter.
Charles E. Cottom.
W.C. Cooke.
James Carson.
H.C. Cady.
John Draper.
B.F. Davidson.
Ozro J. Dodds.
W.B. Dodds.
S.S. Davis.
H.L. Davis.
Lewis Davis.
A.W. Dawson.
Cyrus Douglas.
Hiram DeCamp.
Howard Douglas.
C.B. DeCamp.
C.H. Doughty.
William J. Dunlap.
Edward Dunlap.
Robert E. Dunlap.
J.A. Devin.
F.H. Dugan.

William Doyle.
J.M. Donovan.
R.J. Dalton.
George B. Ellard.
John B. Ellard.
A.C. Edwards.
C.M. Erkenbrecher.
Charles M. Epply.
William H. Epply.
H. Echert.
B.F. Evans.
James C. Ernst.
H.M. Ernst.
R.H. Elias.
A. Franklin.
E. A. Ferguson.
Dr. Z. Freeman.
W. France.
M.S. Forbus.
A.H. Foster.
I.D. Foster.
J.H. Finnegan.
John Findlay.
E.S. Frazer.
W.B. Farrin.
Alfred T. Goshorn.
E.C. Goshorn.
Henry Glassford.
Moses Grant.
James B. Grant.
L.A. Green.
C.P. Griffith.
Griffith P. Griffith.
W.S. Griffith.

From a photo taken at the time. Rufus King, *Center Fielder* Cincinnati Baseball Team, 1868.

W. Austin Goodman.
James N. Gamble.
W.A. Gamble.
Charles H. Gould.
J.B. Guthrie.
T.C. Gaddis.
C. Gillmore.
G.W. Goodhue.
C.C. Gaff.
J.W. Gaff.
Carter Gazlay.
W.S. Groesbeck.
Frank Getty.
Theodore E. Gregg.
Oscar Gregg.
William Greenwood.
R.H. Galbreath.
John Con. How.
George Henshaw.
Murat Halstead.
H.H. Hobbs.
J.L. Haight.
Joseph L. Hal.
W.H. Hall.
W.F. Hall.
Holmes Hoge.
H. Henley.
William Hobart.
J.H. Hunter.
William P. Hulbert.
F.E. Hukill.
Edward W. Hutchins.
J. Huston.
M.B. Hagans.

S.J. Hale.
H.R. Hobbie.
A. Howard Hinkle.
Frank Hinkle.
J.V.B. Hatfield.
A.M. Healy.
J.C. Healy.
J.C. Huntington.
C.L.F. Huntington.
H.D. Huntington.
Mark Hollingshead.
F. Hassaureck.
G. Holterhoff.
Andrew Hickenlooper.
John Holland.
H.F. Heckert.
F.V. Hudson.
Jas. T. Irwin.
J. William Johnson.
Thomas Johnson.
A.G. Jenney.
John P. Joyce.
C.W. Jordan.
L. Jacobs.
N.A. Jeffras.
Rufus King, Jr.
H.L. King.
Samuel L. Kemper.
W.M. Kennedy.
Josiah Kirby.
W.F. Keppler.
Henry Kessler.
A. Keeler.
Nicholas Longworth.

T.D. Lincoln.
A.H. Love.
H.B. Lupton.
C.A. Lockwood.
R.S. Lee.
M.V.B. Lee.
R.W. Lee.
A.S. Ludlow.
W.E. Ludlow.
F.G. Ludlow.
H. Lane.
H.P. Lloyd.
Frank H. Lawson.
Henry Lewis.
James Landy.
John R. McLean.
S.B.W. McLean.
J.E. McLaughlin.
James W. McLaughlin.
George McCammon.
A.F.A. McCord.
J.J. McDowell.
J.J. McCullom.
J.M. McKenzie.
R.H. McKenzie.
William McMaster.
A. McCormick.
C.W. Moulton.
C.E. Marshal.
Stanley Matthews.
C. Bentley Matthews.
Thomas J. Melish.
C.B. Montgomery.
C.E. Malone.

J.H. Mills.
L.E. Mills.
J.M. Macy.
George A. Middleton.
E.C. Middleton.
W.H. Murphy.
H.S. Miller.
H.M. Merrell.
R.F. Morgan.
C.B. Marsh.
W.E. Moore.
J. Wayne Neff.
Peter Rudolph Neff.
William H. Neff.
M.P. Neff.
George W. Neff.
C.H. Nash.
William P. Neave.
Halstead Neave.
Thomas Neave, Jr.
James L. Neave.
W.P. Noble.
Len Norton.
E.F. Noyes.
G. Netter.
J. DeS. Newhall.
J.H. O'Shaughnessy.
Louis O'Shaughnessy.
T.D. O'Donnel.
William Owen.
W.A. Oakley.
George Pickard.
B.P. Pierce.
A.H. Pounsford.

Oliver Perin.
Joseph S. Peebles.
H. Prentiss.
Henry Paul.
George H. Pendleton.
J.L. Pugh.
John D. Pugh.
Harry Pugh.
George W. Pickering.
William Procter.
R.B. Potter.
I.B. Quick.
Charles Rammelsberg.
Frank Resor.
Chas. O. Resor.
I. Burnet Resor.
William Resor, Jr.
F.H. Rollins.
W.E. Rianhard.
S.W. Ramp.
R. Ringwalt.
W.S. Ridgeway.
R.F. Rogers.
J.F. Randolph.
Job E. Stevenson.
Bellamy Storer, Jr.
Edward Stansberry.
C.H. Stevens.
C.K. Schunk.
Charles J. Stedman.
Henry H. Shipley.
Murray Shipley.
C. Shotwell.
W.M. Snowden.

Thomas G. Smith.
W.B. Smith.
James S. Smith.
E.F. Smith.
Earl W. Stimson.
George Shillito, Sr.
Peter Schoenberger.
W.H.H. Small.
Charles Selves.
C.E. Stewart.
W.D. Scott.
David Schwartz.
John L. Stettinius.
J.P. Santmeyer.
William P. Stoms.
Horace Stoms.
C.W. Starbuck.
B.D.Z. Sedam.
H.B. Sinks.
Milton Sayler.
E.B. Seeley.
H.W. Seney.
Charles S. Scanlan.
W.C. Schellinger.
W.P. Thomas.
C.W. Thomas.
J.A. Townley.
Edward E. Townley.
Octavius H. Tudor.
Thomas H. Tudor.
William Torrence.
J.M. Tucker.
Jas. J. Taylor.
W.W. Taylor.

L.M. Thayer.
Eli Terry.
W.C. Townsend.
William Tilden.
Howard Tilden.
Henry C. Urner.
George Vandergrift.
H. Van Valkenberg.
Leon Van Loo.
John C. Whetstone.
William H. Williamson.
Harry Wright.
Benjamin F. Wright.
Nathaniel Wright.
William H. Woods.
John S. Woods.
Drausin Wulsin.
Lucien Wulsin.
R.B. Wilson.
F.E. Wilson.
C.P. Wilson.
H.C. Whiteman.
J.L. Wayne, Jr.

J.H. Walker.
C.S. Walker.
William Worthington.
Edward Worthington.
J. Warfield.
Asa Woodmansee.
F.A. Woodmansee.
F. Wolcott.
E. Wentworth.
J.A. Webb.
I.S. Wise.
Fred Waterman.
Jacob Worth.
J.W. Wilshire.
William B. Wilshire.
D. Wachman.
B.W. Wasson.
B.F. Williams.
D.A. White.
C.C. Winchell.
R.H. Weatherhead.
H.C. Yergason.
H.C. Young.

One cannot refrain from contrasting the game of more than forty years ago with the sport of the present time. The Red Stockings were purely a Cincinnati club. As one of the old patrons of the game remarked to the author, "It would have killed baseball to have brought players from other cities." People looked upon the club as a local institution. The best young men of the city were proud to be members of the club. Men high in the business world were proud to care for the financial end of the team's affairs. In those days, if the baseball patrons had been told that later on the Cincinnati Baseball

Club would be owned and controlled by a man that was not even a resident of the State; that many of the players on the team would be strangers to Cincinnati, hired merely on account of their ability to play the game, while some Cincinnati men would be hired to play on teams representing other cities—what the lovers of the sport in 1868 would have thought of such a proposition is difficult to imagine. They would doubtless have said "that under those conditions the game could not survive a season."

From his last photo taken 1888. Judge Nicholas Longworth, *Member* Cincinnati Baseball Club, 1866–1871.

UNION SKATING POND ON THE GROUNDS OF THE CINCINNATI BASEBALL CLUB.

The baseball season of 1868 having been successfully ended and wound up in a satisfactory manner, there was a meeting of the Board of Directors of the club held on November 4, 1868, at 17½ W. Third Street, with Mr. Alfred T. Goshorn presiding. There were present: Messrs. S.S. Davis, Alfred T. Goshorn, Geo. B. Ellard, Ben F. Wright and Lucien Wulsin. It was decided that the grounds would be rented to the campaign committee of the Union Republican Club for a mass-meeting to be held October 10, 1868, which did much to further the cause in the interest of Grant and Colfax. It was also decided that after this mass-meeting the grounds be banked all around and flooded to prepare for the coming winter skating season. Season tickets for skating were sold at the following prices:

For Lady and Gentleman $7 50
For Lady alone 3 00
For Gentleman alone 5 00
For Child 2 00

The year of 1868 brought forth great excitement in the game of baseball. A number of nines had been formed during the year, and we make mention of some of the most important ones in existence at this time and the players connected with the clubs.

From a recent photo. Dr. Edward W. Walker, *Captain and Pitcher* Indianola Baseball Team, 1868.

THE INDIANOLA BASEBALL CLUB.

Edward W. Walker .... Captain and Pitcher
Horace Stoms .... Catcher
M. Flood .... Shortstop
Guido Egly .... First Base
John Carbine .... Second Base
Thomas Bettens .... Third Base
Mark Lawton .... Left Field
Charles Sweeney .... Right Field
Thomas McAvoy .... Center Field

The grounds of the Indianola Club were located on the present site of the Rookwood Pottery. Lawrence Maxwell was the secretary of the club.

The Great Western Baseball Club, of this city, was quite a strong one, and frequently contested with both the Cincinnatis and the Buckeyes. The players of the nine were:

Bacon	Catcher
Stiles	Pitcher
Black	Shortstop
Arnold	First Base
Holabird	Second Base
Baker	Third Base
Mussey	Right Field
Garlick	Center Field
Siebern	Left Field

On their reserve force were found Messrs. Biggs, Barnes and Mysley.

The Copecs, of Covington, Ky., were a strong club, and very often came on this side of the river to play matches with the Cincinnati and Buckeye Clubs. Interest on the other side of the river was as lively as it was on this side, and, although their nines were not as strong as some in Cincinnati, they, however, played a very good game of ball.

THE COPEC BASEBALL CLUB, OF COVINGTON.

Pearce Barnes	Catcher
Charles H. Thomas	Pitcher
____ Graham	Shortstop
Richard Grant	First Base
James C. Ernst	Second Base
James H. Van Buren	Third Base
____ Beard	Right Field
Thomas Reed	Center Field
____ Camnitz	Left Field

The Baltic Baseball Club was composed mostly of graduates from St. Xavier's College, who put up a good, strong game. Their grounds were in the Millcreek bottoms, near the foot of Gest Street, but these were often played on by a lot of boys who hailed from the West End, and the question of who was to occupy them frequently resulted in a rough-and-tumble fight. Upon one occasion this matter of supremacy was to be finally decided in a contest between the two clubs. The West End boys picked out a tough young lad by the name of Zolar, who was considered by his associates as being able to "whip a barrel of wildcats." The Baltic Club chose Otway J. Cosgrave, the captain and president of the

From a recent photo. Hon. Otway J. Cosgrave, *President and Captain Baltic Baseball Club, 1868.*

Baltics, who could hold up his fists with any youngster that dared to run against him. A circle was formed, and the crowd gathered together to witness the battle. It was a free-for-all game, and "Ott," as the boys called him, gave his opponent such a drubbing that in the future the Baltics held sway, and their right to the ground was ever afterwards undisputed. No doubt this is the first title that our prominent attorney, Otway J. Cosgrave, ever cleared up in a most satisfactory manner. It was by no long-drawn legal process. It was by no moral suasion, but was accomplished by aggressive force, which proved more effective than the most profound arguments or the most finished oratory.

THE BALTIC BASEBALL CLUB NINE.

Thomas F. Shay .... Catcher
James McDonough .... Pitcher
John McCarthy .... Shortstop
William Meyer .... First Base
Jacob Hoeffer .... Second Base
Otway J. Cosgrave .... Third Base and Captain
James Bonner .... Left Field
Patrick Cunningham .... Center Field
Thomas J. Cogan .... Right Field
Louis Stordeur .... Change Pitcher
Augustus Bender .... Change Catcher
J.J. Sullivan .... Umpire
Michael A. Garrigan .... Scorer
M. O'Dowd .... Scorer

Thomas F. Shay was a fine catcher, and when catching behind the bat came into vogue, young Shay adopted this style. He was very successful for a few games, but upon one occasion a very hot ball came towards him which he was unable to hold, and, instead of getting it in his hands, caught it squarely in the eye, which in consequence thereof retired him from his position to lay up for repairs for some days.

THE BUCKEYE BASEBALL CLUB MAKE A TOUR.

The Buckeye Baseball Club also made a tour around the country, playing a number of the best clubs in the surrounding States, and it will be interesting to know what were some of the scores that were made by this club during the year of 1868.

SCORES MADE BY THE BUCKEYE BASEBALL CLUB,
OF CINCINNATI, IN 1868.

			Buckeyes.	Opponents.
May	23.	Red Stockings	10	28
June	12.	Louisville, Louisville, Ky.	28	4
	5.	Athletics, Philadelphia, Pa.	8	22
July	1.	Great Westerns, Cincinnati	83	11
	3.	Railway Unions, Columbus, O.	49	13
	4.	Atlantics, Brooklyn, N.Y.	9	28
	13.	Copecs, Covington, Ky.	53	4
	20.	Detroits, Detroit, Mich.	36	35
	21.	Excelsiors, Chicago, Ill.	43	22
	22.	Atlantics, Chicago, Ill.	28	9
	23.	Forest Citys, Rockford, Ill.	19	11
	24.	Bloomingtons, Bloomington, Ill.	33	17
	26.	Unions, St. Louis, Mo.	25	8
	28.	Empires, Indianapolis, Ind.	44	9
	29.	Actives, Indianapolis, Ind.	64	23
August	11.	Forest Citys, Cleveland, O.	13	8
	23.	Unions, Morrisania, N.Y.	7	12
September	2.	Red Stockings	12	20
	15.	Forest Citys, Cleveland, O.	29	5
	16.	Railway Unions, Cleveland, O.	18	16
	17.	Actives, Indianapolis, Ind.	44	12
	18.	Forest Citys, Cleveland, O.	29	5
	19.	Railway Unions, Cleveland, O.	15	13
	30.	Live Oaks, Cincinnati	40	13

At this time there was a club known as the Cincinnati Amateurs, who were quite active on the field. The following players were found among them: Harry Probasco, pitcher; Harry Wilson, catcher; Miller Outcalt, 2d base; E.W. Walker, 1st; Joe Griffith, 3d; William Miller, shortstop; William Nutt, center field.

Left: From his last photo taken 1902. Charles Davis, *Member* Cincinnati Junior Baseball Club, 1868–1871. *Right:* From his last photo taken 1897. Sir Alfred T. Goshorn, *First President* Cincinnati Baseball Club, 1866–1868. Showing decorations of honor conferred upon him by the crowned heads of Europe and Great Britain.

SIR ALFRED T. GOSHORN

The Cincinnati Baseball Club was particularly fortunate in securing as its first president a man of such intrinsic worth and broad culture as Alfred T. Goshorn. Both Mr. Goshorn and Mr. Champion were representative men in the community, distinguished alike for sterling traits of character, besides being at the same time strong in energy and in executive ability.

With keen wisdom Mr. Goshorn directed the affairs of the

Cincinnati Baseball Club until it stood upon a firm basis. The discipline received from the management as president of the baseball club was of signal service to Mr. Goshorn, who afterwards inaugurated the plans for the annual exhibitions of Cincinnati industry.

As Director General of the Philadelphia Centennial Exposition, much praise and honor were accorded Mr. Goshorn by the Centennial Committee in recognition of his great ability and good management; and as a token of the high esteem in which he was held, he was presented with a handsome library by the citizens of Philadelphia.

He was the only American citizen ever receiving a knighthood, which was conferred upon him by Queen Victoria in recognition of his courtesies to her subjects during the International Exposition, while many other European sovereigns conferred decorations of honor upon him.

Besides enhancing the interests of baseball, General Goshorn was a patron of art, and upon his return from Philadelphia was entrusted with the entire building and furnishing of the Cincinnati Art Museum, and it was owing to his energy and love of the work that Cincinnati stands today as one of the principal art centers in the United States.

It is also to the credit of our city that a man of so much ability was also the patron of our national game, causing it to be recognized as a game worthy of the attention of our most eminent and distinguished men.

◆ CHAPTER IV ◆

*Famous Reds of 1869 and Their Victories—Was the First Professional
Team of the Day—Players Were Secured by a Cincinnatian from All
Parts of the Country—Never Defeated—An Account of Each Player.*

The year of 1869 was an eventful one in baseball in Cincinnati.
It marked the disbandment of the Buckeye Club, the decline of the
Live Oak Club, the elimination of the amateur element among the
players of the Cincinnati Club, and the introduction of professional
baseball here. On April 5, 1869, the Buckeye went into the hands of
a receiver, who was appointed by Judge Taft, of the Superior Court,
to sell off what effects the club had, and it was not long after this
time that the old "Bucks," as they were sometimes called, went out
of existence. The Live Oak Club continued for a short while longer,
when it, also, gave up the ghost.

Previous to 1868 every club in the country was strictly an amateur one, for the laws of the National Association of Baseball Players prohibited the employment of paid players in a club nine, but so
strong was the rivalry between leading amateur clubs of the principal cities, where the game was in full operation, that the practice of
compensating players had worked its way to a great extent.

At the convention of the association held in Washington in
1868 it adopted a new rule, which divided the fraternity into two
distinct classes.

The Cincinnati Club was no exception in the employment of players, for in its nine of 1868 there were four salaried men playing, which, consequently, made it a semi-professional one.

At a meeting of the Cincinnati Baseball Club held September 9, 1868, in the law office of Tilden, Sherman & Moulton, at 17½ W. Third Street, it was decided that if the club desired to have its nine make a good showing in the field during the coming year it would be impossible to do so unless it was greatly strengthened and the amateur element eliminated.

From a recent photo. George B. Ellard, *Organizer* The Famous Red Stockings, 1869.

ORGANIZER OF PROFESSIONAL BASEBALL CLUBS.

Messrs. George B. Ellard and Alfred T. Goshorn were appointed a committee to make arrangements with Harry Wright and his brother George to secure their services for the coming year. George B. Ellard at that time had the largest sporting goods establishment in the West, located in Main Street, below Fourth, and his large acquaintance throughout the country in the baseball world enabled him to choose from the best material for the new nine.

Through the personal efforts of Mr. Ellard he selected and brought together the wonderful Cincinnati Baseball nine of 1869, the "Reds" that made our city famous. He has been properly termed the "Father" of professional baseball clubs.

George Wright, previous to his coming to this city, was playing as shortstop for the Union Club, of Morrisania, N.Y.

Mr. Ellard then sought to secure the services of other first-class players to make up the famous Reds of 1869. He got Andy Leonard and Chas. Sweasy from Newark, N.J. Charlie Gould was the only Cincinnatian on the team. Fred Waterman came from the Mutual Club, of New York City. "Doug" Allison came from Jersey City. Asa Brainard came from the famous Knickerbocker Club, of New York, but he had previously played with other Eastern clubs before coming to Cincinnati. Next to Williams, of the Nationals, of Washington, he was the swiftest pitcher in the United States, and was considered the most graceful and terrific pitcher that had ever gone into the box up to that time. Cal McVey came from Indianapolis.

When the Cincinnatis stepped upon the diamond in 1869 they were the first regular professional baseball nine ever gotten up in the country. Cincinnati can, then, lay claim to being the cradle of professional baseball.

The officers of the Cincinnati Baseball Club in 1869 were:

Aaron B. Champion .... President
Thomas G. Smith .... Vice-President
Col. John P. Joyce .... Secretary
Edward E. Townley .... Treasurer
Drausin Wulsin .... Director
S.S. Davis .... Director
Col. Nicholas Longworth Anderson .... Director
Al. G. Corre .... Director

Harry Wright was chosen as the captain and Oak Taylor as scorer. The nine was composed of the following players:

Harry Wright .... Captain and Center Field
George Wright .... Shortstop
Charles H. Gould .... First Base
Charles Sweasy .... Second Base
Fred Waterman .... Third Base
Douglas Allison .... Catcher
Asa Brainard .... Pitcher
Andrew J. Leonard .... Left Field
Calvin Alexander McVey .... Right Field
Richard Hurley .... Substitute

SALARY LIST.

Harry Wright's all-conquering Reds made a record that will never be equaled in the annals of balldom, and the ten old-timers on the roster only drew $9,300 for their season's work, which was from March 15 to November 15. The salary list was as follows:

Harry Wright $1,200
George Wright 1,400
Asa Brainard 1,100
Fred Waterman 1,000
Charles Sweasy 800
Charles H. Gould 800
Douglas Allison 800
Andrew J. Leonard 800
Calvin Alexander McVey 800
Richard Hurley 600

From photo taken 1869.
Aaron B. Champion,
President.

From his last photo taken 1895.
Thomas G. Smith,
Vice-President.

From photo taken 1869.
Edward E. Townley,
Treasurer.

From photo taken 1869.
John P. Joyce,
Secretary.

Officers Cincinnati Baseball Club, 1869.

Every team in the National and American Leagues today has at least three men who could make the old Red payroll look like a list of stipends of section hands. The good old times may have been all right in their way, but the players of the modern school would prefer the exiting conditions.

HARRY WRIGHT A GREAT CAPTAIN.

Harry Wright, the efficient captain, was always quiet and self-sustained in his demeanor, but he gave his orders with decision, and these were always obeyed implicitly.

In correcting any mistake of his men, he never did it in an offen-

From a recent photo. Hon. Drausin Wulsin, *Director* Cincinnati Baseball Club, 1869.

sive or arbitrary manner. His favorite expression, "You need a little more ginger," acted as effectively as stronger language to infuse an extra amount of vim and action in his players. He was considered the best captain in the world, and a very fine player. To his exertions were greatly due the high playing standard of his nine. Under his careful and skillful management they were trained to work together like a nicely adjusted machine, with no jarring of the different parts. When he played as pitcher his "dew drops" were a mystery to all the crack batters of his time. He never got discouraged, no matter how great the odds were against his club, and by his conduct always inspired his men with confidence in their ability to win. He was not one of the noisy, boisterous kind of captains, but did his work in a quiet, passive way that was far more effective. He was one of the most honorable of men, both on and off the ball field, and highly respected by all who knew him.

THE OTHER PLAYERS.

Douglas Allison was unequaled in the cool and steady manner in which he played behind the bat. When he joined the Red Stocking nine in 1868 he was comparatively unknown to fame, having never played with any prominent club before, but he rose so rapidly that he had no superior. His chief merit as a catcher lay in the manner in which he handled foul tips, the most dangerous kind of batted balls then. He stood directly over the bat, and held them, no matter how hot they came. His running catches of foul flies were beautiful; gracefully, yet surely, did he take them. A pluckier catcher was not be found, or a better thrower to bases. As a batsman "Doug" was first-class, and his red-hot daisy-cutters to left field were hard to stop. Before coming to Cincinnati he was a brickmaker in New Jersey.

Asa Brainard filled his position as pitcher most successfully. He delivered a swift, twisting sort of a ball, and combined a good deal of head work with his physical exertions. He very rarely pitched a ball where the batsman expected it, but sent them in too high, or too low, or too close to the striker, until the latter became nervous or irritated, struck at a ball not fairly within his reach, and "Foul, out," was the usual result. He played his position very neatly, wasting very little time in contemplating the ball (as a great many pitchers did at the time). He watched the bases carefully, and was a very plucky fielder in his position, and was generally sure of all high fly balls.

Charles H. Gould, the only native Cincinnati man on the nine, won the confidence of all the officers of the club. He was one of the best humored men on the ball field, always working with a will, and always to be found at his post. During the season of 1868 he did not miss a single game, nor play in any other position than first base, and was absent but once during the season of 1869. As a first base-man he was one of the best, and, considering the swiftly thrown balls he had to handle, he never-theless got them all. He was familiarly known as "the bushel-basket," for the reason it seemed that no ball that came towards him ever got by, as his far-reach-ing arms and hands were always there to take them in. He was the largest man on the team. Gould's play in the great Mutual-Red Stocking game in New York drew forth the well-merited encomiums of the New York press, for he did not make a single muff (though twelve of the players were put out at first), and made one or two surprising catches. He was a very heavy batsman.

From a recent photo taken expressly for this book. Charles H. Gould, *First Baseman* Cincinnati Baseball Team, 1869.

At second base Charles Sweasy was a reliable and splendid player, who had no superior. Sweasy and his Pythias, Andy Leonard, came from the Irvington Club, of Irvington, N.J., "Sweaz" playing second base in their nine in 1867. The following year he was engaged to play his favorite position on the Buckeye nine in Cincinnati, and his play during that season was so effective that the Red Stockings secured him for their champion nine of 1869. He covered a great deal of territory around his base, and a fly sent to short center or right field was sure to fall into his delicate grasp, as he was one of the surest catchers of high fly balls to be found. He stopped the hottest of grounders without the slightest hesitation, and fielded well to the bases. He watched the game very closely, and took advantage of all chances offered for playing points. He never flinched from a line ball or a thrown one, and was very quick in touching a player out, should a foolhardy opponent try to steal a base on him.

Fred Waterman was very fine and trustworthy at third base. He was an old ballplayer, and formerly played in the Mutual Club in New York City, leaving them in 1868 to join the Red Stockings. He always worked hard to win a game, and was pretty sure of ground balls or foul flies, but his chief merit as a third baseman lay in his beautiful throwing to first, which could not be excelled. He was known as "Innocent Fred" on account of his bland and innocent expression.

George Wright was the model ballplayer in the United States. He could play second and third base in superb style, and he was a fine catcher and change pitcher, but he shone most brilliantly at shortstop, and in this position was unapproachable. He was an old player before he came to Cincinnati, having played with the Gotham Club, of New York; Nationals, of Washington, and Unions, of Morrisania. He covered more ground in his position than any other man in the country, and he and Sweasy made a pair that could not be surpassed. He was as active as a cat, and the way he pounced on a hot daisy-cutter and picked it up, or made a running fly catch, was wonderful. He was much given to indulging in a little by-play, that amused the crowd greatly; yet, though apparently careless, he was always on the lookout, and was sure to cling to any kind of a ball that was sent near enough for him to reach.

Wright was a very swift thrower, and the quickness and dispatch with which he picked up and fielded the ball, often enabled him to make double plays. He backed up the pitcher, second and third base very carefully, and it was not often that a badly thrown ball resulted in any mischief. Take him all in all, George was the very beau ideal of a shortstop. He was the very best batter in the fraternity, and led the score in 1869, not only in his own club, but throughout the country. He struck quickly and with a will, and was very quick in taking advantage of a misplay on the part of his opponents. He delighted in getting caught between the bases when playing a poor club, and his twisting and dodging to escape his pursuers in their frantic attempts to catch him were laughable, and never failed to convulse the crowd. He was also one of the heaviest batsmen, and at stealing bases he was unequaled.

At left field we found that fine player and jolly, good-natured fellow, Andrew J. Leonard, of Irvington-Buckeye fame. "Andy" was a universal favorite and a ballplayer by nature. He played the left field brilliantly, making astonishing catches. He could also play very well in the position of third base, catcher or pitcher. He ranked the best as a batsman.

Calvin Alexander McVey, in the right field, was born in Montrose, Lee Co., Ia., but at ten years of age moved with his parents to Indianapolis. When sixteen years old he joined the University nine there, afterward playing with the Westerns and the Actives. He was engaged for the Red Stocking nine in 1869, and when he made his first appearance in this city, was in a great measure unknown. He, however, improved wonderfully in his play, and at the close of the season he was a first-class player in every respect. His outfielding was very good, as he was a sure catch, a good runner and a fine thrower. His average in batting during the season of 1869 was only second to that of George Wright, which rather astonished the lovers of the game in Cincinnati. "Mc" was also a fine first baseman, and a swift, though a rather wild, pitcher.

At a meeting of the club, held April 5, 1869, resolutions were drawn up on the death of Samuel L. Kemper. He was the first of the club to die, and he had always been a very enthusiastic worker for its welfare. At this same meeting Alfred T. Goshorn sent in his resignation as president of the club, when Mr. Champion succeeded him.

At a meeting, held April 8, at the old Mozart Hall, it was found that the players of the club had reported themselves in good shape, so it was decided to take them on an Eastern tour throughout all the States as far East as Boston, with a challenge to play all comers for the championship of the country. The necessary arrangements were then made to start on Saturday, April 17, but it was later decided to play several practice matches at home, which thereby delayed the start. The first practice game was played with a picked nine, resulting in a score of 24 to 15 in the Reds' favor.

THE OFFICIAL BASEBALL CORRESPONDENT.

Harry M. Millar, son of Cons Millar, the veteran river reporter, was employed by the old *Commercial* to accompany the club during the tour throughout the year as a special correspondent, while at times he acted as scorer. He wrote detailed accounts of all the games and players and telegraphed them to his paper, which was then something unusual, and was considered by many a very extravagant piece of work. His reports and letters were among the best in the country, and he was the recipient of many very flattering comments on the excellent manner in which they were written.

The night before the Reds started on their eventful Eastern tour the playing members of the nine, the substitutes, officers and those who were to be of the party to make the trip assembled at the Gibson House. Under a rule of President Champion, the players were not permitted to leave the hotel, and he personally visited the rooms during the night to see that all the players were in bed getting a good night's rest, that they might be properly fitted for the next day's play.

From an old drawing. Douglas Allison, *Catcher* Cincinnati Baseball Team, 1869.

Mr. Champion stated that the entire Eastern tour was a venture, and much depended upon the gate receipts to help along with the expenses. Mr. Champion had confided these misgivings to several of the members of the club, but each and every one of them assured him that there was no cause for apprehension; that success would surely follow in the wake of the Red Stockings, in whose vocabulary there was no such word as fail. On the strength of these encouraging predictions, the team started the next day, Monday morning, May 31, 1869, with high hope in their hearts and faith in their future victorious achievements. The morning papers came out in great praise of the boys, and prophesied rightly in the remark: "The nine has had plenty of exercise and practice, and is so well regulated that it should avail itself of its capabilities of defeating every club with which it contests."

THE FIRST REGULAR GAME.

It arrived at Yellow Springs, and that afternoon had its first regular game of the tour with the Antioch College nine, defeating it by a score of 41 to 7.

The second game was at Mansfield, O., with the Independents, who were defeated in a score of 48 to 14. From Mansfield they went to Cleveland, Buffalo, Rochester, Syracuse, Albany, Lansingburg, again to Albany, Boston, New Haven, Brooklyn, and thence over to New York to play the Mutuals, which was by far the greatest game of the season.

THE GREAT GAME WITH THE MUTUALS.

They arrived in New York, Monday evening, June 14, at 8 o'clock, all players fresh and in fine condition, rain having prevented their playing a game with the Yale College nine in the afternoon. Another night's rest, in addition to Sunday's and Monday's leisure, brought the players out as fresh as when they left Cincinnati, and when they arrived at the Union grounds in Brooklyn to fill their engagement with the Mutuals, they were as vigorous, athletic and skillful a body of ballplayers as ever stepped over a ball ground. Aware of the great playing strength of the club, the betting men were exceedingly careful as to how they laid their money, considerable money being invested at low rates, while many bets of $100 to $80 and even $75 were quietly picked up.

The threatening state of the weather kept hundreds away from the grounds, but by 2 P.M., when the game was called, it was estimated that over 10,000 people were present, who watched the game with intense interest within the inclosure, while 1,000 more were gathered upon the housetops overlooking the field and at every loophole where a glimpse of the contestants

From a recent photo. George Wright, *Shortstop* Cincinnati Baseball Team, 1869.

could be had. Mr. Chas. Walker, of the Active Club, of New York, was chosen as umpire, and the Reds having won the toss, play was called at 3 o'clock, the Mutuals at the bat.

The Mutuals had defeated the great Atlantics, of Brooklyn, and the Athletics, of Philadelphia, and its nine was considered by all Eastern people as invincible. Among its players was Johnny Hatfield, a former Red Stocking, and the longest ball thrower of his day, a magnificent catcher, fine batter and a general all-around, good player. He had been a great favorite in Cincinnati, but through some misunderstanding left the Reds.

There was much ill-feeling toward him by the Cincinnati nine, and Harry Wright had repeatedly told his team that he wanted them, above all things, to beat the Mutuals, and not allow Hatfield under any circumstances to make a run.

The Cincinnatis, up to the time they played the Mutuals, had defeated everything before them. Entire New York pinned its faith in the Mutuals breaking this record. Excitement was at fever heat. At every place where the individual members went before the game they were jeered and hooted at, the general remark being: "Wait till you play the Mutuals," etc. The day the Reds and Mutuals met was one never to be forgotten by those who witnessed the crowds. The streets for miles were packed with people, afoot and in all kinds of vehicles, going to the grounds, and so dense were the spectators on the grounds that the police were fully an hour pushing them back so there could be room for the players.

While the game was in progress Henry Chadwick, the veteran scorer, and Harry M. Millar, the *Commercial* correspondent, sat under an awning with the players. While there, a man of fine physique and distinguished appearance held a whispered conversation with Chadwick, who turned to Millar and introduced the stranger.

WAS JOHN MORRISSEY.

He was John Morrissey, the pugilist, and afterwards gambler and Congressman. Morrissey closely questioned Millar as to the merits of the players of the Cincinnati nine, and was particular to say several times that he believed Hatfield was on to the plays of all the Reds and that he particularly knew the peculiar change pitching of Harry Wright, and he thought this knowledge would aid the Mutuals to win the game. He asked Millar for his frank and candid opinion as to what he thought would be the result. He told him that he did not for a second doubt that the Reds would win. Then Morrissey referred to the roughness of the crowd, the frequent jeers and cat-calls, and seemed to think that if the Mutuals could not win, the crowd would intimidate the Reds. Millar assured him that no cooler-headed men ever played than the Reds, and Harry Wright never under any circumstances got rattled.

The game went on amid much cheering, but the most intense excitement prevailed in the ninth inning when the Mutuals went to the bat for the last time. Under ordinary circumstances a lead of one run could have been easily overcome, but, playing as the Cincinnatis did, that one run ahead became of vast importance, and, being white-washed seven times in succession, the Mutuals themselves had but little confidence in their ability to win.

When the game ended it was considered the best-played game of ball on record, both nines playing in a style throughout rarely seen. The most extraordinary stops and catches were made, and although the batting was heavy, but few bases were made.

SCORE OF THE GAME.

The great game finished with a score of 4 to 2 to the Reds' favor, and Hatfield never being able to reach first base. The score follows:

Innings	1	2	3	4	5	6	7	8	9
Mutuals	0	0	0	0	0	0	0	1	1—2
Cincinnatis	1	0	1	0	0	0	0	0	2—4

After the game Morrissey said he was a big winner.

Base Ball in Cincinnati

From an old drawings. Asa Brainard, *Pitcher* Cincinnati Baseball Team, 1869. In delivering the ball, Mr. Brainard would cross his legs, placing his left toe on the ground behind his right foot, then take one step forward.

The Cincinnati nine put up at Earle's Hotel in New York, and while there received the following wire from home:

CINCINNATI, June 15, 1869

Cincinnati Baseball Club, Earle's Hotel, New York:

On behalf of the citizens of Cincinnati, we send you greeting. The streets are full of people, who give cheer after cheer for their pet club. Go on with the noble work. Our expectations have been met.

ALL THE CITIZENS
OF CINCINNATI,

Per S.S. Davis.

♦ CHAPTER V ♦

Unbeaten Red Legs of 1869, the Most Famous Ballplayers—Great Reception upon Their Return Home—Official Scores for the Season.

When the news of the victory at Brooklyn reached Cincinnati the excitement was beyond description. Salutes were fired, red lights burned and cheers were deafening. Everybody felt in the finest spirits, and many were willing to lend their friends, and even their enemies, any sum without question. Bands were playing all over town and joy reigned supreme.

After leaving Brooklyn the Reds stopped at Philadelphia, playing the Olympic, Athletic and Keystone Clubs. When the club reached Philadelphia they received the following message:

CINCINNATI, June 21, 1869.

CHAMPION AND JOYCE, C.B.B.C., Bingham House, Philadelphia:

Finest in the world. Predictions true. Imagine two thousand people in and around the Gibson House waiting for the score. Every minute roars and yells go up. Oh, how is this for high?

AL. G. CORRE.

The club, having defeated the Olympics in a score of 22 to 11, the Athletics in a score of 27 to 18, and the Keystones in a score of

45 to 30, then journeyed to Washington, where they played the Nationals and the Olympics. One of these games was viewed by President Grant. While in Washington all the Reds had an interview with the President, who treated them cordially and complimented them on their play. The President smoked all through the interview. They were treated royally by the members of the two clubs, who took them all around the town, showing them everything of attraction and extending to them every possible courtesy. While going around they sang the song:

> We are a band of baseball players
> From Cincinnati City,
> We come to toss the ball around
> And sing to you are ditty;
> And if you listen to the song
> We are about to sing,
> We'll tell you all about baseball
> And make the welkin ring.
> The ladies want to know
> Who are those gallant men in
> Stockings red, they'd like to know.

The Washington papers stated, "The Cincinnati Club drew the most aristocratic assemblage at its games that ever put in an appearance at a baseball match."

The next stop was at Wheeling, W. Va., where it played the Baltic Club, and thence back home, arriving in Cincinnati from its great, successful Eastern tour on Thursday, July 1.

The reception given the players was long to be remembered. They were met by all the members of the club with a band and escorted through the streets, which were decorated on all sides. One firm made a unique design of the letter C of red stockings. Cheer upon cheer went up for the invincible champions, and pandemonium reigned throughout the town. The next day the club played a picked nine for an exhibition game. When the game was completed a wagon drove onto the field with a huge bat, in shape the same as a regular bat, but it was twenty-seven feet long, nineteen inches at the butt and nine and one-half inches at the wrist. On the side was painted "Champion Bat," in gilt, while underneath were handsomely inscribed all the names of the players of 1869.

It was presented by the Cincinnati Lumber Company, and the presentation speech was made by Carter Gazley, the secretary of the company, in which he stated that "the Cincinnati Baseball Club players were recognized as the heaviest batters in the country, and, on that account, it gave him much pleasure to present them with a bat which, although not of regulation size, was not so heavy but that they could easily handle it." He also said that it was not purchased from Geo. B. Ellard, but was grown to order for the occasion.

GRAND RECEPTION.

That evening a large banquet was given the visitors at the Gibson House. The hall was profusely decorated with flags, bunting and flowers. At the head of the hall was a large inscription, "Welcome Home, Red Stockings," with the names of all the players and the officers of the club underneath. Currie's Zouave Band discoursed music, while a sumptuous repast was served. Thos. G. Smith, the vice-president of the club, sat at the head of the table, while on his right was Aaron B. Champion, the president, and on his left John P. Joyce, the secretary. Mr. Smith acted as toastmaster, and when he arose he said: "In addition to the fact that the Cincinnati Baseball Club is the champion of the United States, it is also Champion's club."

From a recent photo. Hon. **Murat Halstead**, *Member* Cincinnati Baseball Club, 1866–1871.

Champion was called upon for an address he made a neat and appropriate speech, and said: "Some one asked me today whom I would rather be, President Grant or President Champion, of the Cincinnati Baseball Club. I immediately answered him that I would by far rather be president of the baseball club." This brought forth loud applause.

Murat Halstead responded to the toast, "The Press." Mr. Halstead remarked that the press was always glad to devote time and space to the interest of baseball, and said that when the returns of the game came in by wire, he had them posted at once on the bulletin board outside of the *Commercial* office, which attracted the attention of great crowds of people, only equaled by those which gathered together during the Civil War times, when the whole country was eager for the latest news. He complimented the nine on their wonderful playing, and said that it took skill, brains, temperance and rigid discipline to accomplish such victories as theirs, which could never be achieved by accident. Alfred T. Goshorn paid a handsome tribute to the players.

Judge Cox responded to "The Judiciary," in which he said, "May there always be impartial umpires in this great game of life."

S.S. Davis, afterwards Mayor of Cincinnati, made a neat address of welcome.

James ("Jimmy") Fitzgerald congratulated the players upon their great success, and said, as they had beaten the Atlantics and also the Bostons, that he hoped their fame and success would spread from the Atlantic to the Pacific. He facetiously remarked that the Bostons had seen that nine spokes of the wheel could defeat the Hub without any trouble.

Last of all Drausin Wulsin covered himself with glory when he arose in response to the toast, "The Ladies, God Bless Them." Upon this subject Mr. Wulsin was fully equal to the occasion. With natural eloquence and chivalric feeling he paid a fitting tribute to the fair sex, which was warmly applauded by all the guests present.

Judge E.F. Noyes, Carter Gazley and Judge Murdock were also among the speakers.

For the next two months the Reds remained at home, playing visiting clubs from both the East and the West.

USED THE ELLARD BALL.

The ball used at this time was the Ellard ball, which George B. Ellard had made for the especial use of the Cincinnati Club.

On July 24 they played the Forest City Club, of Rockford, Ill., defeating them by a score of 15 to 14. In this game A.G. Spalding, now the wealthy merchant of Chicago, acted as the pitcher for the Forest City Club, and was at that time one of the most expert and successful pitchers in the country.

Calvin A. McVey, R. F.; Charles H. Gould, 1st B.; Harry Wright, Captain and C. F.; George Wright, S. S.; Fred Waterman, 3rd B.; Andy F. Leonard, L. F.; Douglas Allison, C.; Asa Brainard, P.; Charles Sweasy, 2nd B. Cincinnati Baseball Team of 1869. From an original photo taken by M.B. Brady in Washington at the time when they played the Nationals.

DISGRACEFUL ACTION ON THE PART OF THE HAYMAKERS.

On August 26 they crossed bats with the Haymakers, or Unions, of Lansingburg, N.Y. At this game occurred the most disagreeable action on the part of a baseball club during the year.

John Brockway, of the Live Oak Baseball Club, of this city, umpired the game. At the end of five innings the score was a tie— 17 to 17. At the opening of the sixth inning, Calvin McVey, of the Reds, went to bat and tipped a ball which bounded three times. Craver, the catcher of the Haymakers, grasped a handful of gravel instead of the ball, and then quickly picked up the ball and held it out at full length for a decision. The umpire decided the striker not out. Fisher, the captain of the Haymakers, ordered the game stopped, upon which a riot almost ensued. President Champion endeavored to argue with the Haymakers, but the crowd grew wild and jumped into the field, causing a great disturbance, and it was only upon the prompt arrival of Chief Ruffin's police that some damage was prevented. It seemed that a number of New York gamblers had placed a large amount of money on the Haymakers, and, fearing a defeat, entered into collusion with the Haymakers to stop the game, under some pretext.

The next evening a special meeting of the Cincinnati Baseball club was held, at which nearly 200 members were present, to discuss the matter. President Champion recommended that the Haymakers' portion of the receipts be withheld until proper amends could be made. It was some months before the rightful apology was received from the Haymaker Club. The papers all over the country commented on this game and stood up for the Cincinnatis in almost every instance. This is the game of 1869 which is recorded as a tie game, but the umpire's decision gave the game to the Reds.

THEIR WESTERN TOUR.

On September 14 the Cincinnati Club made preparations for its Western tour to California. Taking the train that evening, the players reached St. Louis the next day, when they played the Unions of that city, and the following day also defeated the Empire Club. On September 26 they played the Eagle Baseball Club, of San Francisco. They remained there over a week, playing and defeating the Pacifics, the Atlantics and three picked nines. For the sake of variety and amusement they played a game of cricket with the California eleven, in which they showed that they could play cricket as well as baseball, and the Western eleven lost in a score of 18 to 39.

After a most hospitable reception given the club in California, they were escorted to the train in grand style, which they boarded and reached Omaha on October 11, where they played the club there, defeating it by a score of 65 to 1. At this game were present Vice-President Colfax, General Dix and General Auger, then stationed on the Western posts. The next stop was at Quincy, Ill.; Marion, Ind., and then home, coming into the city amid the cheers of the people, while the band played "Hail to the Chief" and "Home, Sweet Home." On October 16th the Athletics, of Philadelphia, met the Reds on the Union grounds back of Lincoln Park in two games, one on the 16th and the other the next day. Both games were in favor of the Reds, one score 55 to 16 and another 17 to 12. The last game and victory of the season of 1869 was played here Saturday, November 5, with the Mutuals, of New York, with whom the most exciting game had been played the June previous. Although the score was not as close as the June game, the Mutuals played well and endeavored very hard to break the unbroken record of the famous Reds of '69, but failed. The score stood 17 to 8.

That evening Mr. Al. G. Corre, the proprietor of the Gibson House, gave a farewell banquet to both nines and the officers of both clubs. This finished the career of the most successful baseball club this country has ever produced. A few offers were made to President Champion by Eastern clubs to have some more games in Cincinnati, but, inasmuch as the grounds were soon to be flooded to prepare for the winter carnivals and skating, the offer could not be accepted.

SCORES MADE BY THE FAMOUS CINCINNATI REDS OF 1869.
NOT ONE DEFEAT.

			Red Stockings.		Opponents.
Apr.	17.	Picked Nine	24		15
	24.	Picked Nine	50		7
May	4.	Great Western, Cincinnati	45		9
	10.	Kekionga, Fort Wayne, Ind.	86		8
	15.	Antioch, Yellow Springs, O.	41		7
	22.	Kekionga, Fort Wayne, Ind.	41		7
	29.	Great Western, Mansfield, O.	35	(3 innings)	5
June	1.	Independents, Mansfield, O.	48		14
	2.	Forest City, Cleveland, O.	25		6
	3.	Niagara, Buffalo, N.Y.	42		6
	4.	Alerts, Rochester, N.Y.	18		9
	7.	Haymakers, Troy, N.Y.	37		31
	8.	Nationals, Albany, N.Y.	49		8
	9.	Mutuals, Springfield, Mass.	80		5
	10.	Lowell, Boston, Mass.	29		9
	11.	Tri-Mountain, Boston, Mass.	40		12
	12.	Harvards, Boston, Mass.	30		11
	15.	Mutuals, New York	4		2
	16.	Atlantics, New York	32		10
	17.	Eckfords, Brooklyn, N.Y.	24		5
	18.	Irvingtons, New Jersey	20		4
	19.	Olympics, Philadelphia, Pa.	22		11
	21.	Athletics, Philadelphia, Pa.	27		18
	22.	Keystones, Philadelphia, Pa.	45		30
	24.	Marylands, Baltimore, Md.	47		7
	25.	Nationals, Washington, D.C.	24		8
	28.	Olympics, Washington, D.C.	16		5
	30.	Baltics, Wheeling, W. Va.	44	(3 innings)	0
July	1.	Picked Nine	53		11
	3.	Olympics, Washington, D.C.	25		14
	5.	Olympics, Washington, D.C.	32		10

			Red Stockings.		Opponents.
	10.	Forest City, Rockford, Ill.	34		13
	13.	Olympics, Washington, D.C.	10	(7 innings)	7
	22.	Buckeyes, Cincinnati	71	(5 innings)	15
	24.	Forest City, Rockford, Ill.	15	(4 innings)	14
	28.	Empires, St. Louis, Mo.	15		0
	30.	Cream City, Milwaukee, Wis.	85		7
	31.	Forest City, Rockford, Ill.	53		32
Aug.	2.	Forest City, Rockford, Ill.	28		7
	4.	Central City, Syracuse, N.Y.	37		9
	5.	Central City, Syracuse, N.Y.	36	(8 innings)	22
	6.	Forest City, Cleveland, O.	43		27
	11.	Riversides, Portsmouth, O.	40		0
	16.	Eckfords, Brooklyn, N.Y.	45		18
	23.	Southern, New Orleans, La.	35		3
	27.	Haymakers, Troy, N.Y.	17	(5 innings)	17
	31.	Buckeyes, Cincinnati	103		8
Sept.	9.	Olympics, Pittsburg, Pa.	54		2
	10.	Alerts, Rochester, N.Y.	32		19

On their California trip they won as follows:

Sept.	15.	Unions, St. Louis, Mo.	70		9
	16.	Empires, St. Louis, Mo.	31		9
	26.	Eagles, San Francisco, Cal.	35		4
	27.	Eagles, San Francisco, Cal.	58		4
	29.	Pacifics, San Francisco, Cal.	66		4
	30.	Pacifics, San Francisco, Cal.	54		5
Oct.	1.	Atlantics, San Francisco, Cal.	76	(5 innings)	5
	11.	Omahas, Omaha, Neb.	65	(7 innings)	1
	12.	Otoes, Omaha, Neb.	56	(5 innings)	3
	13.	Occidentals, Quincy, Ill.	51		7
	15.	Marions, Marion, Ind.	63		4
	18.	Athletics, Philadelphia, Pa.	17		12
	22.	Louisville, Louisville, Ky.	59		8
	24.	Cedar Hill, Cedar Hill, O.	40		10
Nov.	4.	Eagles, Covington, Ky.	40	(6 innings)	10
	5.	Mutuals, New York, N.Y.	17		8

Opposite: From original photos taken at the time in Cincinnati. By Hoag & Co.

CHARLES·H·GOULD
FIRST·BASE

CHARLES·SWEASY
SECOND·BASE

FRED·WATERMAN
THIRD·BASE

GEORGE·WRIGHT
SHORT·STOP

HARRY·WRIGHT
CENTER·FIELD

ANDY·LEONARD
LEFT·FIELD

HARRY·WRIGHT
CAPTAIN

CALVIN·A·McVEY
RIGHT·FIELD

ASA·BRAINARD
PITCHER

DOUGLAS·ALLISON
CATCHER

THE·FAMOUS·

·RED·STOCKINGS.

1869.

Base Ball in Cincinnati

The Reds of Sixty-Nine.
BY HARRY ELLARD.

An old man sat in his easy-chair,
   Smoking his pipe of clay,
Thinking of years when he was young,
   Thus whiling his hours away.

Thinking when he was but a boy,
   So full of mirth and glee,
And we hear him say: "How things have changed;
   They are not as they used to be.

"When I was young, and played baseball
   With the Reds of Sixty-nine,
We then knew how to play the game;
   We all were right in line.

"We used no mattress on our hands,
   No cage upon our face;
We stood right up and caught the ball
   With courage and with grace.

"And when our bats would fan the air
   You bet we'd make a hit;
The ball would fly two hundred yards
   Before it ever lit.

"A home run all could easily make,
   And sometimes six or eight;
Each player knew his business then
   As he stepped up to the plate.

"Let's see! There's Leonard and George Wright,
   And Sweasy and McVey,
With Brainard and Fred Waterman—
   These men knew how to play.

Chapter V

"'Doug' Allison, too, could bat in style,
And so could Charlie Gould.
While Harry Wright oft said with pride,
'My boys are never fooled.'

"This game you see them play today
Is tame as it can be;
You never hear of scores like ours—
A hundred and nine to three.

"Well, well, my boy, those days are gone;
No club will ever shine
Like the one which never knew defeat,
The Reds of Sixty-nine."

In a letter written to the author by Mr. A.G. Spalding, from Point Lomo, California, under the date of September 10, 1907, he gives an interesting account of the famous Red Stockings of 1869:

The old Cincinnati "Red Stockings" of 1869 and '70 have immortalized Cincinnati in a baseball sense, for the wonderful success of that first professional team made its lasting impress on professional baseball. While it naturally stood out prominently as the best baseball club of the period, and while no doubt this prominence was in a great measure due to the fact that it was the only full-fledged professional team in existence at that time, yet no one can gainsay but that the Cincinnati "Red Stockings" of 1869 were a remarkable band of ball players. The two Wright brothers, Harry and George, left their impress on the game; the former for his high principles and managerial ability, as well as being a skillful player; and George on account of his wonderful skill as a shortstop. His skill as a batsman, base-runner, and his attractive figure on the field, have never been excelled. I had a good opportunity to judge of George Wright's skill as a player; I pitched against his team several times while he was a

From a recent photo. A.B. Spalding, *Pitcher* Forest City Baseball Team, Rockford, Ills., 1867–1870.

member of the Cincinnati team, and I was pitcher for the Rockford Club. I also played along with him in the Boston Club from 1871 to 1875, inclusive. His sunny disposition, athletic figure, curly hair and pearly white teeth, with a good-natured smile always playing around them, no matter how exciting the game was, together with his extraordinary skill in all departments of the game, made him in my opinion one of the most attractive and picturesque figures in baseball. I consider him one of the best all-around players the game has ever produced.

I first met George Wright when he was a member of the celebrated National team of Washington, which created such a furor by an extended trip through the West in 1867. I was the young pitcher of the Rockford Club that played against the Nationals in Chicago that year. I shall never forget my peculiar nervous feeling when I first faced "smiling George" in batting position, for the awe in which he and the Nationals were held by all opposing teams was quite enough to set the heart of a young player beating rapidly.

Chapter V

Of course the Nationals thought they had an easy mark with a country club from Rockford, Ill. We had no business to have beaten them, and probably would not have done so, if they had not held us so cheaply in the first part of the game, when they could have gotten in twenty or more runs if they had tried to do so. They looked upon us as an easy thing, and I did not realize there was any chance of the Rockford Club ultimately winning the game, until Mr. Jones, the president of the National team, approached George Wright in an excited manner as he was about to bat, and persuaded him to discard the heavy bat he was about to use and take up a lighter one; a request that George complied with, though evidently it did not altogether coincide with his own judgment.

This incident was an inspiration to the Rockford players as well as myself, and from that moment all fear and timidity vanished, and our team really played good ball for the balance of the game, ultimately winning by the score of 29 to 23. I have always given President Jones much of the credit for the Rockford Club winning that game with the Nationals in 1867.

♦ CHAPTER VI ♦

The Cincinnati Baseball Club of 1870—No Change in Players of the Year Before—Season Opens Very Successfully—Larger Scores Made Than in 1869—Their First Defeat.

The Red Stockings entered the field in 1870 with the same players as the year before, except Hurley was dropped as the substitute and Edward P. Atwater put in his place. The club had settled upon Saturday, April 16, to open the season with a game between the Red Stockings and a picked nine of players from other members of the club, but their expectations in this respect were frustrated by rain. There was also considerable disappointment with the field nine the following Monday when the game was called, as some of the strongest members who had been ready on Saturday did not respond the second day. Among those relied upon, but who were not on hand, were Willard, formerly of the Harvards, but then with the Cincinnatis; Snodgrass, of the Buckeyes; Beckler, of the Great Westerns, and Bellamy Storer and Rufus King, of the Cincinnatis. As it was, the entire field, excepting Meagher (a former Buckeye, but then of the Kentuckies, of Louisville), was made up of the Cincinnati Club. The line-up and the score was as follows:

CINCINNATI.

George Wright .... Shortstop
Chas. Gould .... First Base
Fred Waterman .... Third Base
Douglas Allison .... Catcher
Harry Wright .... Pitcher
Andrew Leonard .... Left Field
Asa Brainard .... Center Field
Chas. Sweasy .... Second Base
Calvin McVey .... Right Field

FIELD.

Prentiss .... First Base
Meagher .... Center Field
Edward Dunlap .... Shortstop
J.W. Neff .... Second Base
E.T. Comergys .... Third Base
Edward Atwater .... Pitcher
J. William Johnson .... Right Field
Joe Marty .... Catcher
R. Ringwalt .... Left Field
J.C. How was the umpire.

Innings	1	2	3	4	5	6	7	8	9
Cincinnatis	2	3	4	2	0	12	2	7	2—34
Field	0	0	0	0	1	0	2	0	2—5

The club then started on their Southern tour, stopping first at Louisville, where they played the Eagles, of that city, defeating them in a score of 94 to 7. They attended the theater in the evening, and the next morning started for New Orleans, where they defeated the Pelicans in a score of 51 to 1; the Southerns, 79 to 6; the Atlantics, 39 to 6 in eight innings, stopped by rain; the Lone Stars, 26 to 7,

From a recent photo. William E. Watson, *Center Fielder* College Hill Baseball Team. 1870.

and the Robert E. Lee's, 24 to 4. A game was to have been played on Sunday, but Harry Wright, finding that the general feeling was against playing on Sunday, did not get his men out. A compliment of which the Cincinnati boys were proud was paid them. A deputation of ministers called and expressed their appreciation, and thanked the officers and players of the club, in behalf of the Christians of New Orleans, for declining the tempting offers to play baseball on the Sabbath, and said they regretted that other Northern organizations visiting New Orleans did not follow the good example set by the Cincinnati Baseball Club.

The club then left for Memphis, playing the Orientals, of that city, on May 4, defeating them badly in a score of 100 to 2. In this game the Redlegs made eleven runs in each of the first eight innings, and in the ninth made twelve runs. The club afterwards came home and played two picked nines, winning in both games. The scores were 37 to 19 and 42 to 17.

They next played the nine of the College Hill Baseball Club, which was composed of the following players:

George A. Wiltsee .... Catcher
James Gladden .... Pitcher
George Hoover .... Shortstop
C. Hammond Avery .... First Base
Harry Colbern .... Second Base
Charles Wild .... Third Base and Captain
William Miller .... Left Field
Walter Davey .... Center Field
Harry Crane .... Right Field

The College Hill team was beaten in a score of 72 to 10. There were also a number of other good players who were members of the College Hill Club, and who did fine work on the ball field. They were: William Watson, Robert Watson, Henry Deininger, ____ Smith, ____ Speed, ____ Eversall, ____ Rogers, Walter Wild.

The Red Stockings then took a flying trip in the near vicinity, playing and defeating the Orions, of Lexington, Ky., 74 to 0; the Unions, of Urbana, O., 108 to 3. This was the largest score ever made by the Reds, and the records stands to this day. They played three games with the Forest Citys, of Cleveland, O., next, defeating them in each game. First, 12 to 2; second, 24 to 10; third, 27 to 18. Coming down towards home, they defeated the Dayton nine, of Dayton, O., with a score of 104 to 9. The Daytons had the following players on their nine:

Harries .... Pitcher
Zink .... Catcher
Brown .... Shortstop
Huckelrode .... Center Field
Martin .... Right Field
C. Mead .... Left Field
Arnold .... First Base

Smith .... Second Base
H. Mead .... Third Base

The Riversides, of Portsmouth, O., were next played, with the usual success; the score was 32 to 3.

By June of 1870 Cincinnati was alive with any number of local organizations among the younger element of our city. Junior baseball nines were being formed everywhere, and during the absence of the senior Red Stockings, the juniors would interest the fans in those

days with games among these local teams. One nine particularly, which they played frequently and which was made up of good players, was called the Ætnas. The players were:

Myers .... Pitcher
Lowery .... Catcher
Traver .... Shortstop
McNulty .... First Base
Maley .... Second Base
Miller .... Third Base
Lowery .... Center Field
Conner .... Right Field
McElroy .... Left Field

George A. Wiltsee, *Catcher* Cincinnati Junior Baseball Team, 1868–1870. *Catcher* College Hill Baseball Team, 1870.

Junior nines were found in Cumminsville, Camp Washington, Carthage, Lockland, Glendale, Tusculum, Riverside, Covington, Newport, Ludlow, White Oak, and, in fact, Junior nines were springing up in all localities.

The Junior Red Stockings of 1870 were made up of the following players, who did excellent work during the whole year:

Smiley Walker .... Pitcher
William Jones .... Catcher
Joe Marty .... Second Base
Ed Dunlap .... First Base
"Pergy" Snodgrass .... Third Base
Harry Colbern .... Shortstop
Ed T. Comergys .... Left Field
Salsbury French .... Right Field
John V. Ellard .... Center Field

THE EASTERN TOUR OF THE REDS OF 1870— THEIR FIRST DEFEAT— FULL ACCOUNT OF THE GAME.

On the first of June began the Eastern tour of the Redlegs, when they stopped on that date to play with the Flour Citys, of Rochester, N.Y. They beat them in a score of 56 to 13, the Cincinnatis making twenty-one runs in the third inning. The Ontarios, of Oswego, N.Y., were next beaten, the score standing 46 to 4. Coming to the Atlantic coast, they defeated the Old Elms, of Pittsfield, Mass.—score, 65 to 9; the Harvards, of Boston, 46 to 15; the Lowells, of Lowell, Mass., 17 to 4; the Clippers, of Lowell, Mass., 32 to 5; the Tri-Mountains, 30 to 6. The players of the Tri-Mountains were:

Sullivan .... Third Base
Record .... First Base
Walters .... Second Base
Sanderson .... Left Field

Jackson .... Pitcher
Pratt .... Shortstop
Huntley .... Catcher
Putnam .... Right Field
Harris .... Center Field

After this game the Cincinnatis were tendered a banquet by the Lowell Baseball Club, of Lowell, Mass. The Fairmounts, of Worcester, Mass., were next defeated in a score of 74 to 19; in this game the Cincinnatis made twenty-three runs in the first inning. They were booked to play the Yale team at New Haven, Conn., but rain prevented them, so they took the train at 4:30 P.M., arriving in New York City in time for supper. The next day they played the Mutuals on the Union grounds in Williamsburg. A morning paper stated that "where there was one person that knew that the Red Stockings were in New York last year, fifty persons knew it this year." It predicted that "the Reds would win all the games played, because the New York nines were not harmonized."

There were over eight thousand persons to see this game, which resulted in a victory for the Reds in a score of 16 to 3. The umpire was Charles Walker, of the Actives, the same who umpired the famous game played with the Mutuals in 1869, and he gave perfect satisfaction.

◆ CHAPTER VII ◆

*The Historic Game with the Atlantics—The Red Stockings Low-
ered Their Banner on the Capitoline Grounds Back of Brooklyn.*

June Fourteenth, Eighteen Hundred and Seventy, is a memorable
date in the history of baseball in Cincinnati. It saw the first defeat of
the most wonderful ballplayers that our city will ever see. The record
of the Cincinnati Baseball Club made in 1869 will never be equaled
in the history of the game. From September, 1868, to June 14, 1870,
the famous Reds played 130 games of ball without one defeat.

Before the game opened, the betting was $1,000 to $200 on the
Reds. At the end of the third inning, when the score stood 3 to 0 in
favor of the Reds, bets of ten to one were offered on their success.
After that inning the tug of war arrived, and the excitement was
deep and painful. The Atlantics were wildly and frantically cheered
for their good plays, while the Reds, of course, when they did something handsome, elicited only sighs and deep groans. The umpire
was Charlie Mills, captain of the Mutuals; his decisions met with
full approval.

At the end of the ninth inning the score stood 5 to 5. Ferguson,
the captain of the Atlantics, proposed to Harry Wright to call it a
draw, and during the conference one of the Atlantics began to carry
the bats to the clubhouse. This caused the large audience of twenty
thousand to leave their seats and close in upon the field.

Base Ball in Cincinnati

Thousands of spectators left the grounds. All of the Atlantics went to their clubhouse near the entrance, and the umpire left the field and got into a wagon near the exit. Some one came and told the umpire that Harry Wright insisted on the game being played to a conclusion, if it took all summer. In this he was backed up by President Champion and Secretary Joyce. The Reds remained at the field, not one of them leaving.

The umpire, finding that Harry Wright was determined to fight it out, left the wagon and summoned the Atlantics back to the field. The umpire and the Atlantics having quit the field, the Reds could have gone also. No point of honor was involved. The Atlantics had said and shown that they had had enough, and the crowd was weary of the intense excitement of the contest. One side was as likely to be victorious as the other, for the Atlantics were heavy and powerful men and displayed no signs of any particular fatigue, and the nerve of both sides was good.

The umpire had told the crowd (half had gone home) that the tenth inning would be played. The field was cleared and the players resumed their extraordinary combat. The tenth inning resulted in a blank for both sides—still a tie. In the eleventh inning the Reds made two runs and victory for them was deemed certain, but the Atlantics batted terrifically—in all, five splendid, safe hits and three runs— their side going out. The instant their captain made the winning run, it thus broke the wonderful charm that had guarded the banner of Cincinnati for two years.

Considering that the Reds played under their average, it would perhaps have been prudent, as it was entirely honorable, to quit at the end of the ninth inning, when the umpire and the Atlantics had left the field. On this point everybody must judge for himself.

The Reds took their defeat good-humoredly, and did not have the slightest idea that the Atlantics could do it again, and for that reason they thought that the Atlantics would decline to play the return game. The defeat was totally unexpected to the club, their adversaries and the public, especially after the Reds' previous day's victory over the Mutuals. Harry Wright said it was a good game, and he was satisfied. President Champion said that he would have played a hundred innings, if necessary to decide the match.

President Champion sent the following dispatch home:

> NEW YORK, June 14, 1870.—Atlantics, 8; Cincinnatis, 7. The finest game ever played. Our boys did nobly, but fortune was against us. Eleven innings played. Though beaten, not disgraced.
>
> AARON B. CHAMPION,
> Cincinnati Baseball Club.

After his return to the hotel that evening, Mr. Champion became so depressed in spirits over the defeat that he wept like a child.

The following interesting account of this game is from the New York *Clipper*:

THE CINCINNATI CLUB IN THE METROPOLIS— THEIR DEFEAT BY THE ATLANTICS— THE FINEST GAME ON RECORD— ELEVEN INNINGS PLAYED—SCORE 8 TO 7 ONLY— AN EXCITING CONTEST IN THE PRESENCE OF TWENTY THOUSAND PEOPLE.

If there is one feature of our national game of ball more than another which especially commends it to popularity, it is the fact of the glorious uncertainty attendant upon it. Hence, no matter how excellent in skill a nine may be, invariable success, season after season, is never at their command; and therefore no club can long monopolize that supremacy which all are ambitious of attaining, for the door is always left open for aspirants to baseball fame to enter the portals of the temple of the goddess and grasp the laurels in the face of the strongest opposition.

Since 1868, the noted "Red Stocking" nine of the Cincinnati Club has escaped defeat in every game they have played up to June 14, 1870, and during that interim they have earned a reputation any club might feel proud of, not only for their masterly displays as skillful experts in the game, but also for their fair and manly efforts to win for the honor of victory, aside from any temptations offered by the dollar and cent influences in the form of extra gate money contests or "betting ring" arrangements. On their third Eastern tour they entered the metropolis victorious in every encounter since they left home, and in their first match with the champion club of New York City they came out of the conflict victorious, after having given our citizens a model display of the beauties of the game of baseball.

On Tuesday, June 14, however, they for the first time met their equals on the field, and after a game played in masterly style on both sides in a majority of the innings, they were obliged to succumb to the superior play of their opponents; but it was a defeat they had no need to be ashamed of, for never before in the annals of the Atlantic Club did the Brooklyn nine make so fine a display of fielding and scientific batting as in this game. Many people supposed that, owing to the great crowd present to witness the Red Stocking and Mutual match, the public desire to see the Cincinnati players would have been satisfied, but apparently the appetite for the Red Stocking displays only grew the faster the more it was fed, for the gathering on the Capitoline grounds on Tuesday exceeded that upon the Union grounds on Monday by at least a third, fully nine thousand people passing into the enclosure of the Capitoline grounds on Tuesday. Without any further preface, however, we now proceed to give the details of each inning's play.

The Game.

The Atlantics very wisely healed all their differences and entered the field in their full strength, and with their eldest and most reliable players in their old positions, including their best batsman, Pearce. Fortunately, too, for their success in the game, a dead ball was provided for the contest, the ball used being a model one for first-class fielding nines. As the Red Stockings entered the field, a few of the roughs in the assemblage attempted to hiss them, but at once a round of applause greeted the strangers, and the hissers were shamed into silence.

Ferguson and Harry Wright selected Charley Mills, of the Mutual Club, as umpire, and a better could not have been chosen. Ferguson, who won the toss, sent the Cincinnatis to bat, and at 3:12 P.M. George Wright took his stand at home base and the game began.

A Parley Between the Contestants.

The game had no sooner reached the close of the ninth inning than one of the directors of the Atlantic Club came on the field and desired Ferguson to close the game as it was; that is, to let it be considered a drawn game. To this Harry Wright demurred, but, despite the calls from the spectators to have the game continued, the Atlantics insisted upon a drawn game, and the umpire, thinking he heard Harry Wright consent, retired from the field; as in such cases, until the two captains of the contesting nines decide what shall be done, the umpire has nothing to say, although he should not leave the field until both captains consent to draw. On consulting the rules in reference to a similar case, it was found that if either captain refused to consent to a tie game at the close of the ninth inning being considered a drawn game, then the party refusing to continue to play loses the game by forfeit, and by a score of 9 to 0. When it was found, also, that the Red Stockings stuck to their posts, and that if the Atlantics did not soon take their places the umpire would declare the game forfeited, Ferguson got his men out again and the game was resumed. As Chapman had taken the bats and marched off the field when a drawn game had been talked of, the crowd rushed in and surrounded the Red Stockings, and considerable "chin music" was indulged in.

THE GAME RESUMED.

The ninth inning had closed at 5:20 P.M., and at 5:25, the field having with difficulty been cleared—the police force present being inadequate for the duty—the game was resumed, the Atlantics again taking their places and the Red Stockings appearing at bat. Gould led off a poor hit, which was captured on the fly by Zettlein; Waterman also passed one up for Chapman to take, but Allison hit a splendid grounder, which the third baseman should not have allowed to go by him; Charley Smith faced the music pluckily and stopped the ball, but could not get hold of it in time to put Allison out, and so the latter secured his base on his hit. There were now two men out and one on base, and Harry Wright came in to send Allison home, but instead he hit a "skyer" for Start to attend to, and away went the

Reds to the field, a whitewashed party for the third time in succession, they having been unable to score since the seventh inning. It was now considered a sure thing for the Atlantics, and after Pike had been caught out by Sweasy, and McDonald and Pearce had earned bases on hits, it was big odds that the Atlantics would win the game. But now it was that the Red Stockings brought strategy into play with brilliant effect, and the way it was done was: Pearce was at first, which he had reached by one of those "fair foul" hits, as they are called, viz.: by hitting the ball close to the base so that it bounds to the foul ball ground back of third base, a hit he tried to make when he struck at the called ball in the fifth inning, this style of hitting almost always ensuring first base, though it is not a showy style of batting—and McDonald was at second, when Smith hit a high ball which fell into George Wright's hands. The base runners, thinking the catch sure, held their bases, but George stooped down so as to take the ball low, and, letting it bound out of his hands, passed it quickly to Waterman at third, cutting off McDonald, forced to run from second; and as Waterman promptly forwarded it to Sweasy, Pearce was thereby cut off at second, and all hopes of the winning run being earned in this inning were at the same time cut off by this beautiful piece of strategic play. The tenth inning closed with the score still 5 to 5. Notwithstanding the disappointment the friends of the Atlantics felt, they nevertheless could not withhold their admiration at the coolness and skill displayed by the Red Stockings in this important period of the game.

THE LAST INNING.

Once more the Red Stockings went to bat, and once more did the Atlantics go to field. Leonard led off with a high ball back of the foul ball line, which Start—who fielded splendidly in the game—caught in handsome style; Brainard, however, hit a long bounder between center and right field, out of Hall's reach, on which he made his second. Sweasy then hit one in the same direction, which Hall got under, and would have held but that McDonald ran against him, and between the two Sweasy secured his first and Brainard reached his third. McVey also hit the ball down Hall's way, Brainard running home the moment the ball was held on the fly by Hall, thereby giving the Cincinnatis the lead in the game once more. George Wright now came to the rescue, and, hitting a hot one toward Pike, secured his base, it being impossible to stop the ball in time. On this hit Sweasy came in, thus leaving the score at 7 to 5 in favor of the Red Stockings, and as Gould was immediately after retired at first by Zettlein and Start, the Atlantics went to the bat with two runs to go to save defeat.

The Final Rally.

It was now evident that Brainard lacked nerve and endurance for such a trial, and apparently the Atlantics perceived this weak spot, for they opened play at the bat with a vim not previously shown in the game. Smith led off with a sharp grounder past third base, which gave him his first easily, and by a high over-pitch of Brainard's he took his third. The applause which followed was stunning. Start followed Smith, and it soon was made evident that Joseph meant business this time, if he never did before, and waiting patiently for a ball to suit him, he sent it flying to right field. As the ball came towards the crowd they gave way, and it fell upon the bankside almost dead. McVey was after it like a flash, but as he stooped to pick up the ball in the crowd one of the partisans present jumped on his back. The crowd did not sympathize with this style of work, and the fellow soon found himself in hot water; in fact, but for the police, he would have been roughly handled. Before McVey could handle and throw the ball, Start secured his third, Smith having preceded him home. Now it was that things began to look lively and promising for the Atlantics. Still, in remembrance of the previous inning's play, there was nothing regarded as sure yet. The point was to avoid George Wright, and, with this point in view, Ferguson, when he went to bat, stood so as to hit the ball left-handed, and, as he can use one hand as well as the other, by this change he drew the ball round from George's reach towards right short, and thereby secured his base on a hit and sent Start home, Joe's run making the score a tie once more—7 to 7. For a minute nothing could be heard for the yells and cheering which resounded from the crowd, but after quiet was partially restored Zettlein went to bat, and, hitting a hot liner to Gould, he made his base, as Gould found the ball too hot and too far out of reach to capture it, but he stopped its force and sent it towards Sweasy. He, however, did not pick it up cleanly, and, in fact, by a bad muff, he not only let Ferguson get his third, but allowed him to steal home, thereby giving the victory to the Atlantics. Hall was the next striker, and as he sent the ball to Sweasy, Zettlein ran for second. But again did Sweasy muff the ball. Pike now came to bat, and, popping up a high one for Sweasy to take, a double play was made, Zettlein being put out on returning to second on the fly ball. This ended the game, with the totals at 8 to 7 in favor of the Atlantics. Below we give the full and correct score:

SCORE.

	Batting.						Fielding.					
CINCINNATI.	O	R	1B	TB	E	L	B	F	LD	T	A	E
G. Wright, s. s.	2	2	3	3	1	2	1	1	0	2	4	0

Gould, 1st b.	6	0	0	0	0	0	8	1	0	9	0	1
Waterman, 3d b.	4	0	2	2	0	1	1	2	0	3	4	2
Allison, c.	2	1	3	3	1	2	0	2	3	5	0	3
H. Wright, c. f.	4	0	1	1	0	1	0	3	0	3	0	0
Leonard, l. f.	5	0	0	0	0	0	0	1	1	2	0	0
Brainard, p.	3	2	2	3	1	0	0	0	0	0	1	3
Sweasy, 2d b.	2	2	3	3	1	1	4	3	0	7	5	3
McVey, r. f.	5	0	0	0	0	0	0	2	0	2	0	0
Total	33	7	14	15	4	7	14	15	4	33	14	12

	Batting.						Fielding.					
ATLANTIC.	O	R	1B	TB	E	L	B	F	LD	T	A	E
Pearce, s. s.	3	2	3	3	1	0	1	0	0	1	2	0
Smith, 3d b.	3	2	2	4	1	0	0	2	0	2	0	1
Start, 1st b.	3	3	3	5	0	0	8	6	0	14	0	0
Chapman, l. f.	4	0	0	0	1	0	0	2	0	2	0	0
Ferguson, c.	3	1	2	2	0	1	0	2	2	4	0	3
Zettlein, p.	5	0	1	1	1	0	0	2	0	2	1	0
Hall, c. f.	5	0	1	1	1	0	0	2	0	2	1	0
Pike, 2d b.	4	0	1	1	0	1	1	1	0	3	6	1
McDonald, r. f.	4	0	1	1	1	0	0	2	0	2	0	2
Total	33	8	14	18	5	2	10	20	2	33	9	7

Runs scored	1	2	3	4	5	6	7	8	9	10	11
Cincinnati	2	0	1	0	0	0	2	0	0	0	2—7
Atlantic	0	0	0	2	0	2	0	1	0	0	3—8
Runs earned	1	2	3	4	5	6	7	8	9	10	11
Cincinnati	0	0	0	0	0	0	2	0	0	0	0—2
Atlantic	0	0	0	0	0	0	0	1	0	0	2—3

Of the play in this remarkable contest, where all did so well, it would be almost invidious to select any individual player for special

Opposite page: From photos taken at the time. **Athletic Baseball Team, 1870. F. G. Malone, C.; A. J. Reach, 2nd B.; W. D. Fisler, 1st B.; J. Radcliff, S. S.; J. T. Pratt, 3rd B.; J. D. McBride, P.; G. Bechtel, L. F.; J. Sensenderfer, C. F.; Thomas Berry, R. F.; H. C. Schafer, R. F.**

praise, but Ferguson's splendid catching on one side, and George Wright's model shortfielding on the other, certainly merit praise-worthy remarks. Smith's third-base play, too, was a model display, and assuredly neither Start nor Pike ever played their positions bet-ter, while Pearce's nerve and judgment, and his skillful, scientific play at the bat, was of valuable service to the Atlantics. Zettlein never pitched with such effect as in this game. The fact that such a nine as the Red Stockings have were put out in eleven innings' play for two earned runs is sufficient to show the character of the pitching of Zettlein in the match. Brainard was equally effective up to the tenth inning, but afterwards he fell off. The out-fielding of the Red Stockings was a feature in their play, the cleverness displayed in judging the batting of the Atlantics being especially noteworthy. The clubs were fortunate in having an umpire who proved himself thoroughly impartial and sound in his judgments, both clubs being fully satisfied with him, and this is rarely the case. The game was played in a thoroughly friendly spirit by the contesting nines.

THE RETURN MATCH WITH THE ATLANTICS.

The Atlantics did play the return match when they visited Cincinnati the following September 2, when they lost the game to the Reds in a score of 4 to 3. On October 26 the Red Stockings vis-ited Philadelphia and played the decisive game with the Atlantics, when they were again defeated by the Atlantics in a score of 11 to 7. The defeat of the Reds by the Atlantics two out of three games played with them, thus made the Atlantics champions for the year of 1870. Had the present-day rules been in vogue at that time, the Reds would have won the pennant with a large percentage.

THE RED STOCKINGS' GAME
WITH THE ATHLETICS.

On June 17 the Red Stockings defeated the Eckfords, of New York, in a score of 24 to 7. Leaving New York, they then went over to New Jersey, where they defeated four clubs; Thence to Philadelphia, where they encountered and won from the Intrepids, Keystones and Athletics. The Athletics were a strong team, and the city was alive with excitement and interest over their contest with the Red Stockings. There had been immense crowds out to see ball games before, but on this day (June 22, 1870), neither in regard to the number of people nor the intense interest in the game, had any previous contest in Philadelphia, or in the country, ever equaled the gathering assembled to witness this game, and for excitement no contest of any kind in the sporting annals of the Quaker City had up to that time ever equaled it.

The players of both nines were as follows:

CINCINNATIS.

George Wright .... Shortstop
Allison .... Catcher
Brainard .... Pitcher
Gould .... First Base
Sweasy .... Second Base
Waterman .... Third Base
Harry Wright .... Left Field
Leonard .... Center Field
McVey .... Right Field

ATHLETICS.

Radcliff .... Shortstop
Malone .... Catcher

Base Ball in Cincinnati

McBride .... Pitcher
Fisler .... First Base
Reach .... Second Base
Pratt .... Third Base
Bechtel .... Left Field
Sensenderfer .... Center Field
Schafer .... Right Field

The Athletics presented the name of Mr. Holbach, of the Keystones, and the Reds nominated Mr. Glover, of the New York Empires, to act as umpire. Neither seemed to be satisfactory, so a compromise was made on Mr. McMullen, who had recently joined the Haymakers. He acted with great impartiality and was satisfactory to both the public and the players. The game started at 3:45 P.M., and lasted three hours and twenty-five minutes. The score made:

Runs Scored	1	2	3	4	5	6	7	8	9
Cincinnati	2	2	4	5	5	3	4	0	2—27
Athletics	7	4	1	3	1	1	4	4	0—25

The Athletics were a more powerful club than the Atlantics, and as they had defeated the latter the Monday previous, 19 to 3, they considered a victory over the Red Stockings as almost beyond a doubt. Philadelphia was jubilant over that 19 to 3, and offered odds on its favorites. It had been arranged to ring the State House bell the night of the game over the triumph of the Athletics, but, alas! the joyous peals came not forth.

The Reds played with a splendid coolness and nerve that was worthy of the highest admiration. The game opened strongly against them, but they went to work and pulled up, and pulled ahead with a power and courage that convinced the multitude that the Red

Stockings battled as well as when they were behind as when they were ahead.

At the end of the second inning, when the score was 11 to 4 against the Reds, it was thought, of course, that another defeat was in store for them. The Athletics got this lead by terrific batting. They furnished the most elastic ball they could get, and the manner in which they sent it flying beyond the outfielders in the first and second innings promised very bad for the Cincinnatis.

The eighth inning closed with a tie—25 to 25—over which the multitude were wild with joy, for their favorites had caught up by a splendid chance hit that brought two men home, and gave the striker a home run. The ninth inning closed the battle, and closed it gloriously, with the only blank for the Athletics, and leaving Fisler, their best player, at third. The multitude groaned as the concluding fly rested in George Wright's hands, and then dispersed very quietly.

The Cincinnatians present were very jubilant. They cheered and threw up their hats, and waved handkerchiefs. There was some attempt made by the Philadelphians to carry Allison off the field on their shoulders, but the red-legged catcher declined that sort of transportation. The Reds rode to and from the grounds in an omnibus drawn by four horses decorated with a number of flags. On the way out the small boys shouted, "You're a-goin' to get beat," "You're a-goin' to get beat." Coming back, the men waved their hats and the women their handkerchiefs, while the bad small boys looked up with chagrin and said "Go to hell."

CHAPTER VIII

Homeward Bound—The Red Stockings Presented with Banner.

After leaving Philadelphia, the Red Stockings stopped at Baltimore and Washington, reaching home after their great Eastern tour on July 1st. Their first encounter here was on July 2d, when they played a very close game with the Forest Citys, of Rockford, Ill., however winning the game in a score of 14 to 13, but two days afterwards they defeated this same club in a score of 24 to 7. The 9th of July, when the Reds visited Rockford, the Forest Citys played a tie game with them, 16 to 16. The Kekiongas, of Fort Wayne, Ind., met the Reds on the 13th of July, and this date seemed to prove a hoodoo, for the Reds beat them in the game with a score of 70 to 1. In the seventh inning of this game the Reds made twenty-seven runs.

On July 27 the Cincinnati Club suffered their second defeat, when they were matched against the Athletics, of Philadelphia. The Reds did their best, but they finally succumbed to the visiting club in a score of 7 to 11.

On August 16 there was held a meeting of the members of the Cincinnati Baseball Club at Mozart Hall, to transact the usual business of the month. At this meeting the resignations of President Aaron B. Champion, Vice-President Thomas G. Smith and Secretary John P. Joyce were read and accepted with most profound regret. These gentlemen had given to the club much of their time during the previous year, but their business was such that they would not be able to devote any more time away from it. The success of the Red Stockings of 1869 was greatly due to the energy, enthusiasm, ability, brains, hard work and the time devoted by Mr. Aaron B. Champion and Mr. John P. Joyce, all of which was given by them without any compensation whatever. After quite a lengthy debate, new officers were chosen and elected. Mr. A.P.C. Bonte was the President; Mr. Al. G. Corre, Vice-President, and Mr. W.P. Noble, Secretary.

The White Stockings, of Chicago, were the next ones to shatter the prestige of the Red Stockings, when, on September 7, they defeated the Redlegs in a score of 6 to 10; this was their third defeat. Just previous to this game, on the 2d of September, the Reds defeated the Atlantics, of Brooklyn. It will be remembered that this club had given the Reds their first defeat, but on this day the Reds won in a score of 14 to 3. When the game was over, Mr. Aaron B. Champion came out upon the field and presented the Red Stocking players with a handsome silk banner a gift from the ladies. Mr. Champion said in his speed:

"*Gentlemen of the First Nine of the Cincinnati Club*:—I have the honor, on behalf of a number of ladies of our city, to present to you this beautiful banner. These ladies desire in this token to express to you not only the pleasure they have felt in witnessing your play, but also wish to testify their approbation and delight that you have made the word 'Red Stocking,' which is placed on this flag, famous throughout the country by your gentlemanly qualities, as well as by your abilities on the field. They hope that your conduct will hereafter be as pure as the color of this flag on which the name is written, and that no stain shall ever be put upon it by your actions, but that it may remain white and unsullied as now."

To this presentation speech Harry Wright responded:

"On behalf of this nine, I wish to say to these kind givers of this flag, that we sincerely thank them for this gift, and also thank them for the kind feelings (thoroughly appreciated by us) which induced it. We shall always carry this banner with us, and, though it may not on every occasion float over a victorious ball field, yet it shall ever wave over us as victors over all temptations." (Applause.)

October 13 was the next unlucky day for the Reds, for they were again defeated by the White Stockings, of Chicago, in a score of 13 to 16. On the 15th the Red Stockings suffered their fifth defeat of the year, when they laid down to the Forest Citys, of Rockford, Ills. The score was 5 to 12.

The Atlantics, of Brooklyn, who had won and lost a game with the Reds, were matched against them on October 26, to decide the best two out of three. The sixth and last defeat of the Reds came then. They played another 7 to 11 game, as they did when they lost to the Athletics on July 27.

The last game of the year of 1870, and the last game in which the old Red Stockings, the heroes and champions of the year of 1869, ever played together, was played with the Forest Citys, of Cleveland, O. And the Reds won the game with the score 28 to 5.

When the Reds stepped out of the field after the conclusion of this game, their end was near at hand. The Executive Committee and the officers of the Cincinnati Baseball Club who had followed Mr. Champion, Mr. Smith and Mr. Joyce had adopted new rules and regulations by which the club was to be governed in the future. Public interest and enthusiasm had greatly weakened. People were no longer willing to put up the money to sustain the club in the way in which it should be. The players became dissatisfied, and it was quite evident that the nine and the club would soon be broken up.

Chapter VIII

SCORES MADE BY THE CINCINNATI BASEBALL CLUB
DURING THE SEASON OF 1870.

			Red Stockings.		Opponents.	
Apr.	18.	Picked Nine, Cincinnati	34		5	
	21.	Eagles, Louisville, Ky.	94		7	
	25.	Pelicans, New Orleans, La.	51		1	
	26.	Southerns, New Orleans, La.	79		6	
	28.	Atlantics, New Orleans, La.	39	(8 innings)	6	
	29.	Lone Stars, New Orleans, La.	26		7	
	30.	Robert E. Lees, New Orleans, La.	24		4	
May	4.	Orientals, Memphis, Tenn.	100		2	
	6.	Picked Nine, Cincinnati	37		19	
	7.	Picked Nine, Cincinnati	42		17	
	8.	College Hills, Cincinnati	72		10	
	12.	Forest Citys, Cleveland, O.	12		2	
	13.	Forest Citys, Cleveland, O.	12		2	
	20.	Riversides, Portsmouth, O.	32		3	
	23.	Orions, Lexington, Ky.	74		0	
	25.	Unions, Urbana, O.	108		3	
	26.	Daytons, Dayton, O.	104		9	
	31.	Forest Citys, Cleveland, O.	27		13	
June	1.	Flour Citys, Rochester, N.Y.	12		2	
	2.	Ontarios, Oswego, N.Y.	46		4	
	3.	Old Elms, Pittsfield, Mass.	65		17	
	4.	Harvards, Boston, Mass.	46		15	
	6.	Lowells, Boston, Mass.	17		4	
	8.	Clippers, Lowell, Mass.	32		5	
	9.	Tri-mountains, Boston, Mass.	30		6	
	10.	Fairmounts, Worcester, Mass.	74		19	
	13.	Mutuals, New York City, N.Y.	16		3	
	14.	Atlantics, Brooklyn, N.Y.	7		8	lost
	15.	Unions, Morrisania, N.J.	14		0	
	16.	Resolutes, Elizabeth, N.J.	22		7	
	17.	Eckfords, New York City, N.Y.	24		7	
	18.	Stars, Brooklyn, N.Y.	16		11	
	20.	Amateurs, Newark, N.J.	53		2	
	21.	Intrepids, Philadelphia, Pa.	52		14	
	22.	Athletics, Philadelphia, Pa.	27		25	
	23.	Keystones, Philadelphia, Pa.	37		26	

Base Ball in Cincinnati

			Red Stockings.		Opponents.
	24.	Pastimes, Baltimore, Md.	30		8
	25.	Marylands, Baltimore, Md.	30		8
	27.	Olympics, Washington, D.C.	35	(8 innings)	25
	28.	Nationals, Washington, D.C.	30		10
July	2.	Forest Citys, Rockford, Ill.	14		13
	5.	Forest Citys, Rockford, Ill.	24		7
	9.	Picked Nine, Cincinnati	56		19
	11.	Forest Citys, Rockford, Ill.	16		16 tie
	13.	Kekiongas, Fort Wayne, Ind.	70		1
	16.	Eagles, Louisville, Ky.	25		13
	18.	Harvards, Boston, Mass.	20		17
	27.	Athletics, Philadelphia, Pa.	7		11 lost
	30.	Mutuals, New York City, N.Y.	15		12
Aug.	5.	Indianapolis, Indianapolis, Ind.	61		8
	6.	Olympics, Washington, D.C.	38		3
	9.	Haymakers, Troy, N.Y.	34		8
	22.	Live Oaks, Cincinnati	45		2
	23.	Amateurs, Washington, C.H., O.	72		6
	27.	Riversides, Portsmouth, O.	29		27
Sept.	2.	Atlantics, Brooklyn, N.Y.	14		3
	7.	White Stockings, Chicago, Ill.	6		10 lost
	15.	Riversides, Portsmouth, O.	12		1
	21.	Resolutes, Hamilton, O.	36		4
	27.	Empires, St. Louis, Mo.	7		5
	28.	Unions, St. Louis, Mo.	28		1
Oct.	6.	Forest Citys, Cleveland, O.	18		15
	13.	White Stockings, Chicago Ill.	13		16 lost
	15.	Forest Citys, Rockford, Ill.	5		12 lost
	24.	Haymakers, Troy, N.Y.	12		7
	25.	Mutuals, New York City, N.Y.	7		1
	26.	Atlantics, Brooklyn, N.Y.	7		11 lost
Nov.	2.	Mutuals, New York City, N.Y.	23		7
	5.	Forest Citys, Cleveland, O.	28		5

GAMES OF THE CINCINNATI RED STOCKINGS IN 1870.

	Cincinnati	Opponents.
Number of games played	74	74
Number of games won	68	6
Total number of runs	2,732	648

MR. AARON B. CHAMPION.

From his last photo, taken 1894. Aaron B. Champion, *President* Cincinnati Baseball Club, 1869.

Aaron B. Champion was the second president of the Cincinnati Baseball Club. He was a man of the highest integrity in character, and possessed a courteous and genial manner which endeared him to each member of the club. His was a noble nature, which never swerved in his faithfulness to duty and in his devotion to high principle.

No club with such a man as Mr. Champion at its head could ever be recreant to the high standards which he established for its regulation, and much of the success of the Cincinnati Club was due to his excellent management. At his death the following telegram from the president of the Baseball League, received by Mr. Ren Mulford, Jr., at that time baseball reporter for the *Post*, speaks for itself as an indication of the general high regard in which Mr. Champion was held:

WASHINGTON, D.C., September 3, 1895

I am pained to hear of the death of my old friend. He was not only Champion in name, but champion of everything that was honest and clean in baseball. The League will take suitable action, expressive of its deep regret and its appreciation of his manly, noble and honorable character, when it meets.

N.E. YOUNG, President.

◆ CHAPTER IX ◆

*The Dissolution of the Old Red Stockings and Disbanding of the
Original Cincinnati Baseball Club.*

The nine of 1869, as has been seen, played all through the following year without a change in its players, but by the end of the season it became quite evident that they could no longer hold together. Professional baseball players had crept into almost every club of note in the country. The old Reds were offered increased salaries, much more than the people of Cincinnati would be willing to contribute.

The players of the unbeaten Reds of 1869 then sought entrance into other clubs in the East, many of them joining the Boston Baseball Club, while others joined the Olympic Baseball Club, of Washington, D.C.

The end of the year 1870 marks the breaking up of the Cincinnati professional Red Stockings, until they were reorganized under an entirely new system and management some years later. This fact will be observed by the reading of the following circular sent out by the president of the Cincinnati Baseball Club, Mr. A.P.C. Bonte, which bears the date of November 21, 1870:

> DEAR SIR:—According to the custom, the Executive Board reports to the members of the CINCINNATI BASEBALL CLUB its determination in reference to the baseball season of 1871. We have had communication with many of the leading baseball

A.G. SPALDING
PITCHER

HARRY WRIGHT
CENTER

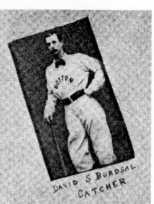

DAVID S BURDSAL
CATCHER

CHAS. H. GOULD
FIRST

GEORGE WRIGHT
SHORT

CALVIN A. McVEY
CATCHER

ANDREW LEONARD
LEFT

FRALEY V. ROGERS
RIGHT

HARRY C. SHAFER
THIRD

ROSS C. BARNES
SECOND

players throughout the country, as well as with the various members of our former nine.

Upon the information thus obtained, we have arrived at the conclusion that to employ a nine for the coming season, at the enormous salaries now demanded by professional players, would plunge our club deeply into debt at the end of the year.

The experience of the past two years has taught us that a nine whose aggregate salaries exceed six or eight thousand dollars can not, even with the strictest economy, be self-sustaining.

If we should employ a nine at the high salaries now asked, the maximum sum above stated would be nearly doubled. The large liabilities thus incurred would result in bankruptcy or compel a heavy levy upon our members to make up a deficiency. We are also satisfied that payment of large salaries causes jealousy, and leads to extravagance and dissipation on the part of the players, which is injurious to them, and is also destructive of that subordination and good feeling necessary to the success of a nine.

Our members have year after year contributed liberally for the liquidation of the expenses incurred in the employment of players. We do not feel that we would be justified in calling upon them again; and, therefore, for the reasons herein stated, have resolved to hire no players for the coming season. We believe that there will be a development of the amateur talent of our club, such as has not been displayed since we employed professionals, and that we will still enjoy the pleasure of witnessing many exciting contests on our grounds. We take this opportunity of stating that our club and grounds are entirely free from debt; and, deeming it our first duty to see that they remain so, we pursue the course indicated in this circular.

For the Executive Board,

WILL. P. NOBLE, Secretary.　　　A.P.C. BONTE, President.

Opposite: **From original photos taken by Warren in Boston at the time. Boston Baseball Team, 1871–1873.**

Shortly after the above circular was sent out, there was a called meeting at the residence of one of the officers, when it was decided to disband the club. A public meeting of the members was then held and this decision was put into effect. And so it was that the great baseball club which has made our Cincinnati the cradle of our professional national game, passed out of existence, to live only in the memories of those enthusiastic lovers of the sport who can, during their hours of reminiscences, recall the time when they were young and cheered for the old Red Stockings in the days of "Auld Lang Syne."

THE REDS INVADE ENGLAND.

The year of 1874 was memorable in baseball by the trip of the Boston and Athletic Clubs to England. The clubs left Philadelphia on the steamship "Ohio," July 16, arriving in Liverpool on July 27. Among the players of the Boston Club were Harry Wright, George Wright, Cal McVey, Andy Leonard, Sam Wright (the brother of Harry and George Wright), and Al. G. Spalding, who is today so well known in the baseball world.

Baseball games were played at Liverpool, Manchester, London, Sheffield and Dublin. The Englishmen were greatly astonished at the wonderful celerity of the baseball players in fielding. The scores of the games were large, owing to the speedy grounds played upon.

CLUB MANAGEMENT.

Mr. John P. Joyce, the secretary of the Cincinnati Red Stockings of 1869, was the first one to initiate a system of management into

The Cincinnati Baseball Park, Showing Diamond.

a baseball club, when he piloted that wonderful team in their unparalleled successful trip from ocean to ocean.

The victories achieved by the Red Stockings in this year aroused such great interest and enthusiasm among the general public in the game of baseball, that the following year more than a score of cities throughout the country followed the example set by Mr. Joyce in the employment of a regular manager to keep their teams in good discipline and under proper training.

FORMED AN ASSOCIATION.

The success of the Red Stockings of 1869 led to the organization of other nines of that class, and by 1871 the clubs had become numerous and influential enough to establish a professional association of their own. On March 17, 1871, the first convention of delegates from representative professional clubs throughout the country was held at Collier's Café, corner of Broadway and Thirteenth Street, New York City, when the National Association of Professional Baseball Clubs was formed.

In that year the first series of championship contests under a regular official code of rules was established, and since then the professional contests have been the most interesting baseball events of each season.

Upon the establishment of the National League of Professional Baseball Clubs, the Cincinnati Club fell into the hands of George and Josiah Keck, who moved the grounds from the rear of Lincoln Park to those near the Stockyards. They were afterwards moved to the foot of Bank Street, and thence to their present location.

THE CINCINNATI BASEBALL CLUB OF 1876.

J.L. Keck .... President
G.H. Van Voorhis .... Secretary
David P. Pearson .... Catcher
William C. Fisher .... Pitcher
Charles H. Gould .... First Base
Charles J. Sweasy .... Second Base
A.S. Booth .... Third Base
Henry Kessler .... Shortstop
Charles W. Jones .... Left Field
Robert Clark .... Center Field
Emanuel Snyder .... Right Field
Samuel J. Fields .... Substitute

CHAMPIONSHIP CLUB, 1859–1876.

1858–9   New York. (Picked Nine from New York Clubs.)
              Fashion Course Games.
1860   Undecided.
1861   Brooklyn, of Brooklyn.

1862	Eckford, of Brooklyn.
1863	Eckford, of Brooklyn.
1864	Atlantic, of Brooklyn.
1865	Atlantic, of Brooklyn.
1866	Athletic, of Philadelphia.
1867	Unions, of Morrisania.
1868	Athletic, of Philadelphia.
1869	Cincinnati RED STOCKINGS.
1870	Atlantic, of Brooklyn.
1871	Athletic, of Philadelphia.
1872	Boston, of Boston.
1873	Boston, of Boston.
1874	Boston, of Boston.
1875	Boston, of Boston.

Ever since the Cincinnati Baseball Club has belonged to the League of Professional Baseball Clubs, it has endeavored each year to land the pennant, but has time and again failed to get the cherished trophy. It is difficult to say why such has been the case, so we must attribute it to bad luck.

Foreword

My readers have seen by the preceding pages that the Cincinnati Baseball Club was broken up at the close of the year of 1870, and was not reorganized until the formation of the National League of Professional Clubs in 1876.

It will, I know, be of great interest to many of my friends to learn something of baseball since that time to the present day, from the pen of one who is thoroughly conversant with the subject.

My lifelong friend, Mr. Ren Mulford, Jr., has kindly consented to give us this information in the subsequent pages.

Mr. Mulford is too well known in the baseball world of today to need any introduction. His long connection with the Cincinnati *Enquirer*, Cincinnati *Times-Star* and the Cincinnati *Post* as

Ren Mulford, Jr.

their baseball editor, as well as his many able and well-written contributions to their columns, has won for him a national reputation,
while his articles as a baseball correspondent for *Sporting Life* have
been conceded as among the best in the country.

It is with much pleasure that I publish, in connection with my
early history of the national game, Mr. Mulford's *resumé* of the sport
in Cincinnati from 1876 to the present time.

CHAPTER X

The Ball Fields from 1876 to the Present Day.

The fact that the prophet Isaiah mentioned ball-tossing in his chronicles of the days of the ancient Hebrews rather adds to the bemuddlement of Henry Chadwick, A.G. Spalding, W.M. Rankin, John Montgomery Ward and the other historians who have been throwing the searchlight of investigation into the past, vainly hunting for the birthplace of baseball.

All authorities agree on the one point that Cincinnati was the cradle of professional baseball. The famous Red Stockings of 1869 was the first paid team in baseball history, although the spirit of commercialism had crept into the game before that period. Some of the "stars" of the amateur teams around the country in the late sixties enjoyed clerkships that came to them on account of their ability to play the game, rather than in recognition of their business gray matter. Two years before the organization of the National League in 1876, the Centennial year of our independence, two American teams, the Bostons and Athletics, made a tour of England and gave

John Bull his first glimpse of the sport destined to become our great American national game. Since that first invasion of foreign land, diamond missionaries have spread the clean gospel of American sport the world over. Base hits have been made in the shadow of the Pyramids in Egypt and on soil of the Caesars. There are in existence today baseball leagues in Hawaii, Australia, Japan, the Philippines, South Africa, England, Cuba and Porto Rico. Every one of Uncle Sam's warships is provided with a baseball equipment, and the crew of every cruiser and battleship lays claim to a baseball team, and, in fact, baseball follows the flag everywhere.

To attempt to tell the story of baseball from the days of 1866 to 1907, a space of thirty-two eventful years, would be to grind out MSS. that could not be squeezed into the covers of a volume as pretentious as an encyclopedia. The roll-call of the immortals of the diamond would in itself be a stupendous task, for in every city where baseball is played, some baseball hero has pitched, batted or fielded himself into sporting history.

Thirty-two years of baseball. A lifetime of the sport. Were it possible to muster all of the professionals, major and minor, who have taken part in the championship of those three decades and two years of diamond activity, a great army in knickerbockers would be gathered together that would require hours to pass a given point.

Perhaps it is odd that Cincinnati, the cradle of the game, should now be "The Hague of Baseball." It would not be out of place to call the body, which is popularly described as the Supreme Court of Balldom, the National PEACE Commission. Since the days of '76 baseball has had its bloodless wars in which fortunes have been lost struggling for players and territory.

The National League came into existence in 1876, and was "Cock of the Baseball Walk" until the first American Association was organized and took the field six years later in 1882. The National,

From a recent photo. Hon. August Herr-mann, *Director* Cincinnati Baseball Club. *Chairman* National Commission.

while not hostile to the stripling, was not especially joyous in its welcome, but in 1884 the first great cloud fell athwart the baseball horizon, when the Union association took the field with chips on both shoulders. Recognizing no rights of territory or reservation, the Union association planted its guns in the stronghold of both National League and American Association, but one year's conflict sufficed and the colors of the Union Association were lowered in defeat.

Two years after A.G. Spalding had taken the Chicagos and All Americas around the world—the great event of 1888—the rebellion of the Players' Brotherhood occurred. Stars deserted to the Players' League in battalions, and the National League found itself in the thick of the conflict, not for supremacy, but for existence. For this fight of 1890, the National League was strengthened by the accession of the Cincinnati and Brooklyn Clubs. The defection of these clubs likewise weakened the American Association. The Players' League found the National League a tough foe, but at the close of 1890 the old organization was virtually on the ropes. The Cincinnati Club had been sold to the Players' League emissaries. In the ranks of the latter organization, however, an epidemic of cold feet occurred and the Nationals outgeneraled their opponents, who retired from the field, and a new National Agreement was accepted in which the old Boston Players' League Club became a member of the storm-tossed American Association, which had also suffered heavy financial reverses during the stormy fight of '90.

That dream of peace in baseball, however, was short-lived. The American Association, reinforced by Boston and Washington, balked on the decision of Allen W. Thurman and Colonel John I. Rogers, comprising the majority in the Board of Control, awarded Harry Stovey to Boston and Louis Bierbauer to Pittsburg, players claimed to be on the Athletics' reserve list. Louis C. Krauthoff, the Western Association member of the board, dissented from this majority opinion, which was responsible for a tremendous uproar in the American Association camp. Immediate rebellion resulted, in which Colonel Thurman was deposed and the new National Agreement shattered, while Cincinnati was taken into the American Association. That was the last act which prefaced the war of 1891. The lions and the lambs in this struggle met at Indianapolis in the winter of that year, and most of the Association lambs were swallowed in the amalgamation that brought the Twelve-club League into the field, but the "meal" cost $181,000 in good, hard cash. The National League worried along the major way with a dozen clubs in each championship race until 1900, when Cleveland, Washington, Louisville and Baltimore were retired by outright purchase. This left the field in control of one big eight-club organization, which was soon compelled, however, to notice the aggressive youngster, under Ban Johnson, which had begun life as the Western League. Cleveland, abandoned by the National, was taken into the new American League circuit, and permission granted to put a second club in Chicago, under Charles

A. Comiskey. Thus the American League came into prominence as a factor for recognition as an equal of the National League. The expansion microbe was at work in the American body politic. The American's friendly overtures for a foothold in the East met with silence on the part of the National League. Meanwhile the old American League territory had been awarded to the new American Association, which, under Thomas Jefferson Hickey, was looming up in the West. Cut out of their old stronghold, the American abandoned Kansas City, Indianapolis, Minneapolis and Buffalo, and added Boston, Philadelphia, Baltimore and Washington to their circuit. That was the signal for the last war of 1901-'02, the fiercest fought of all baseball conflicts.

The abandonment of Milwaukee a year later gave St. Louis a rival. The wrecking of the Baltimore Club in mid-season of 1902 had no effect upon American lines. The playing breach was patched up, Baltimore continued in the League, but in December the Orioles were dropped and New York admitted in the place of the Marylanders.

In the meantime "Fandom" was tired of contract-breaking and all the displays of fractured faith that had been seen in all baseball wars. The advent of August Herrmann and his Cincinnati associates, Julius and Max Fleischmann and George B. Cox, into the councils of the National League was responsible for brighter days in the old organization. They were good fighters, but they saw no common sense in the throat-cutting warfare. Cincinnati has been the scene of many historic baseball occurrences. Victorious teams have been welcomed home by brass bands and great concourses of enthusiasts. The "Big Four"—August Herrmann, Julius and Max Fleischmann and George B. Cox—however, who acquired the Red Club from John T. Brush and Ashley Lloyd by purchase, was celebrated by a tremendous night parade, in which tons of red fire were burned. The

streets were thronged with cheering "Bugs," and at a downtown
dinner the new magnates were received with acclaim. This mid-season deal has been pronounced the
tonic which saved the National
League. Cincinnati new blood un-
doubtedly prevented the game from
going to ruin, and in the winter of
1902, at New York, emissaries of
peace from the National were welcomed with open arms by the
American League. On January 10,
1903, the Cincinnati peace compact
was signed, and thus ended the last
of the diamond wars. Yet, in spite
of these periods of unrest, interest
in the game itself continued to increase.

From a recent photo. Col. Max
C. Fleischmann, *Director* Cincinnati Baseball Club.

THE HAGUE OF BALLDOM.

These cited upheavals were not the only periods of unrest in
balldom by any means. A dozen organizations for the propagation
of peace in balldom have lived and died, and the National League
in the summer of 1903 gave the minor leagues an opportunity to get
together and enjoy home rule and self-government when they abro-
gated at Redbank the national agreement from which the American
League had withdrawn. The establishment of the National Commission, with August Herrmann as president—chosen by Harry Pulliam,

of the National League, and Ban B. Johnson, of the American League—and John E. Bruce, secretary, was the happiest event of a decade in balldom. The National Association of Professional Base-ball Leagues, of which Patrick T. Powers is the president, at once came under the wing of the National Commission in friendly affilia-tion with the ruling powers of the two major leagues. When Secre-tary John H. Farrell called the 1907 roll of members of the National Association, no less than thirty responded. The full roster is as fol-lows:

Eastern League.	Western Association.
American Association.	South Atlantic League.
Southern League.	Texas League.
Pacific Coast League.	Ohio-Pennsylvania-Maryland.
Western League.	Western Pennsylvania League.
New York League.	Cotton States League.
New England League.	Northern Copper.
Connecticut League.	Iowa State League.
Tri-State League.	Kansas State League.
Central League.	South Central League.
Indiana-Illinois-Iowa League.	Wisconsin League.
Northwestern League.	Gulf Coast League.
Ohio-Pennsylvania League.	Western Canada.
Virginia League.	Eastern Illinois.
Inter-State League.	South Michigan.

The admission of the Pacific Coast and Tri-State Leagues was the greatest stroke of the past few years for the betterment of orga-nized baseball. These actions closed the gates to the derelicts and made contract-jumping unprofitable. The amount of capital tied up in professional baseball now runs into the millions. An army of pro-fessional players are today drawing good salaries. The increase in the compensation paid for baseball talent over the output in the early days is enormous. The Cincinnati Club paid Manager Ned Hanlon alone more money in 1907 than all the Red Stockings of '69 drew for the never-to-be-equaled record, while his salary was almost as large as that which the entire champion Reds of 1882 drew for winning the only pennant ever credited to a Cincinnati team in a regular championship race, the first year of the American Association. Today there are thirty-four leagues under the jurisdiction of the National Commission, with an aggregate of 4,500 players under contract, earning in salaries each year the sum of $3,500,000. At least $8,000,000 are invested in professional baseball, while each small city has from twenty-five to fifty small league clubs. In addition, nearly every county in the more densely populated States claims a league. Uncle Ben Shibe, the veteran of the baseball business, manufactured over 5,000,000 baseballs last year.

CINCINNATI IN THE BASEBALL WARS.

During the troublesome times in baseball, Cincinnati has been in the thick of the struggles. League Park, which is now the site of the "Palace of the Fans," the most magnificent structure ever dedicated to baseball enthusiasts, was once upon a time an old brickyard near Western Avenue, with ponds of various sizes, where the boys would amuse themselves wading and throwing mud at each other.

The Reds of '76, under Josiah L. Keck, were at home on the old Avenue grounds beyond the Stockyards, which were reached by special trains from the old Plum Street Depot, or by a long, tedious ride on the old horse-cars. Later on the Bank Street grounds were secured. There the ill-fated National League team under Nathan Menderson played. It was here that the Reds of 1882 were victorious in the first campaign of the American Association. Aaron S. Stern was the mogul who directed Cincinnati's only flag-winners. Louis Kramer, the attorney, was the President; Louis Herancourt,

From a recent photo. Hon. Julius Fleischmann, *Director* Cincinnati Baseball Club.

Treasurer, and the late O.P. Caylor, one of the most brilliant baseball historians the game ever knew, Secretary. Charlie Fulmer was the manager and Charles N. Snyder, field captain. William H. White and Henry McCormick did the pitching, with Snyder and Phil Powers behind the bat. The others were: Dan Stearns, First Base; John A. McPhee, Second Base; W.W. Carpenter, Third Base; Charles Fulmer, Shortstop; Joe Sommer, Left Field; Jimmy Macullar, Center field, and Harry Wheeler, Right Field. Harry Luff played twenty-seven games at first base.

Cincinnati won fifty-four and lost twenty-six games that year, and beat the famed Eclipse Club, of Louisville, ten games. This was before the day of world's championships, but that fall, on the Bank Street lot, the Reds, under Captain Snyder, met the Chicago League champions and Captain Anson, and divided honors in a brief two-game series. White had the better of Fred Goldsmith, and McCormick lost to Larry McCormick. Cincinnati, the cradle of the professional game, was thus the scene of the first clash between champions in major leagues.

When the Union Association slipped into the field in 1884, the Cincinnati Club, with Justus Thorner, President, Frank B. Wright, Secretary, and George Gerke, Treasurer, euchred the American people out of the Bank Street grounds. Colonel Stern simply hustled and secured the plot on Western Avenue between Findlay and York, turned the old brickyard and truck garden into a ball field, and got several squares closer to the center of the fan population. Neither Red Club made a barrel of money that year, but the Unions were badly beaten in the race for patronage.

Nine years later a Cincinnati man succeeded Allen W. Thurman as the American Association president. Louis Kramer led the American warriors that year. John T. Brush and Ashley Lloyd were in command of the Red division of the National League that season of 1891, and the opposition "King Kel's Killers," managed after a fashion by Michael J. Kelly, were located far out of drawing distance at the Gymnasium grounds in the East End. During the season the Pendletonians deserted "Fort Ed. Renau" on the Ohio River, and found refuge in Milwaukee. The next year, 1892, Frank Bancroft, who had been the business manager of the Killers, began his National League career with the Cincinnati Club—one of continued integrity and sterling worth. The Nationals thus gained about all worth counting as spoils of the two years of war.

CINCINNATI IN THE GAME.

Cincinnati was a member of the National League the year of its organization in 1876, and came very nearly losing all its games, suffering fifty-six defeats and gaining but nine victories. Ross Barnes was the Hans Wagner and Napoleon Lajoie of that day, and he led the heavy batting division with a credit of .403. Hon. Morgan G. Bulkeley, afterward the Governor of Connecticut, was the first president of the National League, and his successor was W.H. Hurlbert, the Chicago man who saved the game during the dark days of 1877 when A.H. Nichols, William H. Craver, George Hall and James A. Devlin were found guilty of "throwing" games, while members of the Louisville Club. They suffered expulsion and were never reinstated. After Hurlbert came "Uncle Nick" Young, the faithful. Cincinnati was officially dropped out of the National League in 1877, although a scrub team played the schedule through, but the games did not count in the championship. Cincinnati finished second in the race of 1878, fifth in 1879, eighth and last in 1880.

The season of 1880 was not a financial success, except to the Chicago Club, and this result was largely due to the enforcement of the half-dollar tariff for admissions. For the first time in the history of the League up to this date, no club had disbanded before the League season ended, and neither had the season's play been disgraced by the retirement of any team from the field on account of alleged unfair decisions by the umpire. The full record of the games played showed Chicago in the van, with Providence occupying second place, and Cleveland third. The struggle for fourth place was close, but Troy won it, and though Boston tied Worcester for fifth place, the latter won by having the fewer defeats and best percentage of victories, leaving the Bostons occupants of sixth place for the first time in ten years. Buffalo stood seventh and

From a recent photo. Hon. John E. Bruce, *Secretary-Treasurer* The National Commission.

Cincinnati last. Seven drawn games were played, and the Cincinnati Club had three games unfinished, one each with Worcester, Troy and Buffalo. All the other clubs played their full schedule out.

Cincinnati was a member of the American Association from its first inception in 1882 to 1889, inclusive, and has been in the National League from 1890 to the present day. In the winter of 1891 the Association and the National League were amalgamated at Indianapolis. During these years J. Wayne Neff, John Hauck, George Herancourt and Harry Sterne at various times figured in the ownership. In many of the games the best known exponents have worn the color made famous by the team which Harry Wright directed in 1869. William Buckingham Ewing, perhaps the greatest catcher the game ever knew, never realized his ambition in winning a pennant for Cincinnati, but during his *regime* the Reds were "up there" and fighting in all save his last managerial year. "King Bid" McPhee's playing career began when he helped win the flag of 1882, and he was renowned as a second baseman beyond compare. Michael J. Kelly—"King Kel"—began his major career "out on the Avenue," and came back in the days of his decline. Old Hoss Radbourne, Frank Bancroft's right bower the year Providence cantered away with the National pennant, rounded up his major playing career in Cincinnati. So virtually did Charles A. Comiskey, the Old Roman, who has won world's championships for both St. Louis and Chicago; Louis Rogers Browning, the "Gladiator;" Parisian Bob Caruthers, Curt Welch, Arlie Latham, Tip O'Neill and Joe Kelly.

The champions during the life of the old American Association were—

1882	Cincinnatis.
1883	Athletics, of Philadelphia.
1884	Metropolitans, of New York.

1885	St. Louis.
1886	St. Louis.
1887	St. Louis.
1888	St. Louis.
1889	Brooklyns.
1890	Louisvilles.
1891	Bostons.

Captain Comiskey was the manager of the four-time winners, the Brown Stockings, of St. Louis.

CHAMPIONS—NATIONAL LEAGUE.

	CLUB.	MANAGER.
1876	Chicago	A.G. Spalding.
1877	Boston	Harry Wright.
1878	Boston	Harry Wright.
1879	Providence	George Wright.
1880	Chicago	A.C. Anson.
1881	Chicago	A.C. Anson.
1882	Chicago	A.C. Anson.
1883	Boston	John Morrell.
1884	Providence	Frank Bancroft.
1885	Chicago	A.C. Anson.
1886	Chicago	A.C. Anson.
1887	Detroit	W.H. Watkins.
1888	New York	James Mutrie.
1889	New York	James Mutrie.
1890	Brooklyn	W.H. Connigh.
1891	Boston	Frank Selee.
1892	Boston	Frank Selee.
1893	Boston	Frank Selee.
1894	Baltimore	Ned Hanlon.
1895	Baltimore	Ned Hanlon.

1896	Baltimore	Ned Hanlon.
1897	Boston	Frank Selee.
1898	Boston	Frank Selee.
1899	Brooklyn	Ned Hanlon.
1900	Brooklyn	Ned Hanlon.
1901	Pittsburg	Fred Clarke.
1902	Pittsburg	Fred Clarke.
1903	Pittsburg	Fred Clarke.
1904	New York	John J. McGraw.
1905	New York	John J. McGraw.
1906	Chicago	Frank Chance.
1907	Chicago	Frank Chance.
1908		
1909		
1910		

MORRIS H. ISAACS.

("The King of the Fans.")

There are men in this world so modest in advancing their own claims that they stay so far in the background that there is no room for them to cast a shadow. When the cause of somebody else appeals, however, you will find them in the forefront beating the cymbals and tom-toms with a six-cylinder energy.

Redland is notable all over balldom for its fete days. Take out those for which Morris H. Isaacs is largely

From a recent photo. Casper H. Rowe, *Director* Cincinnati Baseball Club.

♦ 175 ♦

Morris H. Isaacs.

if not wholly responsible, and not very many would be left. A confessed Bug—filled with enthusiasm and the spirit of helpfulness, Mr. Isaacs richly deserves the crown of "King of the Fans." His has been a kingdom of action. Years ago the Reds were crippled beyond seeming recovery. They went East with Phil Ehret as the only available pitcher in form. Nobody expected them to do more than prove door-mats upon which the Eastern sextette could wipe their spiked feet. Ehret, the Red, proved his worth. He won victory after victory, pitching out of his turn, and showing such a spirit of loyalty that Cincinnati went baseball mad. It was Morris H. Isaacs who devised a welcome home for Ehret and the Reds.

A band, a great crowd of cheering enthusiasts, a parade in carriages on Fourth Street, proved a sequel to Mr. Isaacs' idea, that was only the forerunner of other affairs, some of them assuming the rank of national importance. The benefit to Harry Wheeler, of the '82 champions; the John A. McPhee Day; the presentation to Charles E. Irwin and his bride, and the marvelous success of the Harry Weldon Day, all these are credits due Morris H. Isaacs. He supplied the ideas and the needed energy to carry them out. The celebration which marked the *entree* of the Herrmann-Cox-Fleischmann *regime* was another affair devised by Mr. Isaacs, and carried out with such enthusiastic fervor that the glare of red fire and rockets lighted all balldom.

◆ CHAPTER XI ◆

Fete Days at Cincinnati Ball Park— The Cincinnati Baseball Club of Today.

HARRY WRIGHT DAY.

During the first part of the year 1896 it was proposed to have one day set aside in many parts of the country to be known as Harry Wright Day. This was for the purpose of raising a fund for the erection of a suitable monument over the grave of the former idol of the baseball world.

The day was observed in Boston, Cincinnati, Philadelphia, Louisville, Baltimore, Washington, Detroit, New York, Rockford, Ills., Kansas City, Indianapolis and Derby, Conn. Games were played in each of these cities, and the receipts were devoted to the Harry Wright Memorial Fund.

April 13, 1896, was the day selected, and although the weather was rather cold for ballplaying, the amount collected was a neat sum.

Cincinnati celebrated the day with a game at the grounds between the team of Ninety-six and the team of Eighty-two. Many of the old-time fans turned out to witness the game, and "Doc." Draper, of the original Cincinnati Baseball Club, J.R. Brockway and John Boake, of the old Buckeye Baseball Club, acted as umpires. It ended in a score of 7 to 3 in favor of the team of '96. The players of both the nines were as follows:

1896 TEAM.

Frank Dwyer .... Pitcher
"Buck" Ewing .... First Base
Henry Peitz .... Catcher
"Germany" Smith .... Shortstop
Billie Gray .... Second Base
Charley Irwin .... Third Base
"Dusty" Miller .... Right Field
"Bug" Holliday .... Left Field
Eddie Burke .... Center Field

1882 TEAM.

Will White .... Pitcher
John Reilly .... First Base and Right Field
Charley Snyder .... Catcher
Charley Fulmer .... Shortstop
"Bid" McPhee .... Second Base
"Hick" Carpenter .... Third Base
Charley Gould .... Right Field and First Base
Jack Shoupe .... Left Field
Joe Sommers .... Center Field

In the evening a large banquet was held at the Gibson House for the two teams and their friends. Mr. Henry Chadwick, the veteran baseball correspondent, was the guest of honor, and appeared upon the field in practice "stunts."

JOHN (BID) A. MCPHEE BENEFIT.

During the early part of the spring of 1897 Morris H. Isaacs, so well known in the local baseball affairs, conceived the idea of getting up a benefit for John A. McPhee, then the second baseman of the Cincinnati Reds, in commemoration of the fifteenth consecutive season of faithful services as a member of the Cincinnati team, so that it would render it possible for him to make the final payment on his house and lot.

Mr. Isaacs, through his untiring efforts, interested every fan in town, besides the members of the Cincinnati Chamber of Commerce, who took an active part in the event. A committee was formed, which sent out the following notice through the columns of the *Enquirer*:

To the Lovers of the National Game in Ohio, Indiana and Kentucky—

It is the intention of the baseball enthusiasts of Cincinnati to present to John A. McPhee, of the Cincinnati Reds, a fitting testimonial of his long and honorable career upon the diamond, and in view of the fact that there are so many loyal rooters in the three above-named states, the undersigned committee in charge of the affair desires that every city and town in Ohio, Indiana and Kentucky should be represented upon the occasion, and call upon those who look with favor upon the proposition to start subscriptions to be known as their contributions to the tribute that will be paid to one of the grandest ball players that ever donned a uniform, and a player whose credit to the national game is second to none in the world. All contributions forwarded to the sporting editor of the Cincinnati *Enquirer* will be duly acknowledged.   Respectively,

SAM BAILEY, JR., *Chairman,*

THOMAS J. COGAN,   TONY HONING,

E.O. MCCORMICK,   MORRIS H. ISAACS.

After this circular had been announced in the paper, contributions began to pour in, not only from Cincinnati, but from all parts of the country. Tony Honing was the first to start the ball rolling with $50.00; W.W. Peabody then came forth with a liberal check, and next came N. Ashley Lloyd, with $100.00. Checks of one dollar and upwards came in from all points in the three states mentioned, besides from other states, so by the time the day had arrived for the celebration quite a liberal sum had already been subscribed.

Thursday, July 29, 1897, was the day set for the game to be played between the members of the Cincinnati Chamber of Commerce and a nine made up from the newspaper men in town. This game marked an epoch in local baseball. It was an echo of the ancient Roman and Greek times, when the victors of the Olympic games were crowned with laurels, and when physical manhood was the highest acme to which ambition attained. The celebration was opened by a big street parade, which started at 12:30 P.M., in which all the notables took part. The pageant was made up as follows:

Police.
The only and original Chamber of Commerce Band.
The Zoo Opera Singers.
Zara, the Juggler.
Players in carriages.
Newport and Covington enthusiasts.
Lagoon Band.
Japs.
Masters Robert Boyer and Albert Hays, Trick Bicycle Riders.
Elephants and Camels.

When the parade reached the ball park there was a unique exhibition of the Lagoon Japs, who were kindly sent with the compliments of Mr. Noonan, the manager of that popular resort. There was then an exhibition of fancy trick bicycle riding by Masters Robert

Boyer and Albert Hays, who were only five and ten years of age. A splendid entertainment followed by the Zoo Opera Company, which was gratuitously sent by the Zoo management.

When McPhee appeared upon the diamond to umpire the game of the day, he received a rousing ovation that was very affecting. Morris H. Isaacs then presented him with a splendid souvenir from the wives of the Cincinnati Redlegs. It was a silver toilet set, beautifully ornamented and carved. Then began the game of the day between the Chamber of Commerce nine and the newspaper team. The line-up was as follows:

CHAMBER OF COMMERCE MEN.		NEWSPAPER MEN.
Rudel	Catcher.	Strauss
Allen.	Pitcher	Assur
Deagle	Shortstop	Doran
Fetter	First	Grillo
Romer	Second	Zuber
Eagen	Third	Schwartz
Ransick	Left	Holmes
Mappes	Center	Wald
Garner	Right	Anthony

Lingo for the Chamber of Commerce and Taylor for the newspaper men played as extra men.

THE SCORE.

Innings	1	2	3	4	5	6	7	8	9
Newspaper	4	2	1	2	2	4	6	6	0—27
Chamber of Commerce	0	0	0	1	0	1	0	6	1—9

Umpire, John A. McPhee.

Base Ball in Cincinnati

From photo taken at the time. Top Row—W.C. Phillips, P.; Billy Gray, 2nd B.; Harry Vaughn, C.; Tom Parrott, P.; Billy Rhines,P.; Harry Spies, C. Center Row—"Bug" Holliday, C. F.; "Bid" McPhee, 2nd B.; Billy Merritt, C.; Morgan Murphy, C,; Wm. "Buck" Ewing, 1st B. and Captain; W.E. Hoy, L. P.; Chas. E. Miller, R. F.; George Smith, S. S.; Frank Dwyer, P. Bottom Row—Frank Foreman, P.; W.A. Latham, 3rd B.; George Hogriever, O. F. Trilby the Mascot. The Cincinnati Baseball Team, 1895.

The Chamber of Commerce Band, led by Major Rufus Burck-hardt, played interludes between the innings, and were forced by their own sense of the appropriateness of things, to play the Dead March for their own team after those awful seventh and eighth innings.

At the end of the third inning Morris H. Isaacs opened the doors of the ball park to all of the youngsters who were hanging on the outside, and who did not have any money for their admissions.

The affair was in every way a great success, due to the energy of Morris H. Isaacs, and the amount realized from the contributions and the receipts of the game was $1,908.000, which was handed to Biddy McPhee, who was overwhelmed in his appreciation of what had been done for him.

HARRY WHEELER GETS A BENEFIT.

Harry Wheeler, who was the crack right fielder of the Cincinnati Baseball Team in 1882 (the year that our boys won their only pennant when members of the American Association), had retired from his activity on the ball field and had entered into a business life. Later on he became prostrated with locomotor ataxia, which rendered him helpless, with a wife and two children dependent upon him.

This fact had come to the notice of Morris H. Isaacs, who at once determined to help his old friend in every way possible. He immediately started a subscription list among his friends and the local baseball fraternity. This occurred during the spring and summer of 1898, and by the fall of the same year the amount realized from the various contributions reached the splendid sum of $1,525.00.

This amount Mr. Isaacs took to former Mayor John D. Caldwell, asking him to select a custodian of it, and to pay to Mrs. Wheeler in such monthly installments as he deemed best. Mayor Caldwell left the selection to Mr. Isaacs, who chose Aaron S. Stern, the president of the Cincinnati Baseball Club during the year of 1882, when Harry Wheeler played.

Mr. Stern paid the money over to Mrs. Wheeler in monthly installments of $35.00 until the whole amount was exhausted, which was surely a godsend to the old-time right fielder. Harry Wheeler died October 9, 1900.

CHARLIE IRWIN'S WEDDING PRESENT.

During the later nineties Charlie Irwin played third base for the Cincinnati Team, and he most certainly put up a great game.

At the opening of the season he had informed his friends that he had concluded to take a partner for life. During the middle of the season the Cincinnati Team left for their Eastern tour, to be gone some weeks. While they were away Morris H. Isaacs conceived the idea of making Charlie a wedding present when he returned to Cincinnati. To this end Mr. Isaacs started a subscription list, with a limit of twenty-five cents—no more, no less. Some desired to give more, but their contributions were not received above the desire sum. Mr. Isaacs started out with his list, and from time to time, as the list grew, he pasted the sheets together, so by the time it was completed, it contained 753 names, and reached to the length of twenty feet. This list was nicely pasted on muslin and bound with red edges, and the amount raised was $188.25.

After much discussion, it was finally decided to give the money in gold, which was placed in a neat plush bag. At the first game played by the club after their return, when Charlie Irwin came to the bat and took his place at the plate, Judge Howard Ferris, who made the presentation speech, walked out on the field, followed by Mr. Isaacs' little four-year-old boy, Stanley M. Isaacs, dressed in white and red, carrying the plush bag and its contents. Judge Ferris, in a few very fitting remarks, presented the old third baseman with the bag of gold, with a wish from all of his friends that he would live to enjoy a long and happy life.

The extensive list was gotten up in a nice roll and presented to Irwin a few days later.

HARRY WELDON DAY AT THE PALACE OF THE FANS.

Harry Weldon, the "prince of sporting writers," was, previous to the time he was stricken with paralysis (which was on Sunday morning, February 25, 1900), the sporting editor of the Cincinnati *Enquirer*, where he began his duties during the stifling days of the torrid July of 1881. In all the years that followed up to the time he was stricken, Harry Weldon served the *Enquirer* and John R. McLean with untiring faithfulness. He was one who was better known between the two oceans than half of the statesmen who have sat in the halls of Congress during all the years that he was a faithful chronicler of the affairs of the diamond, mat, track, field and ring. Loyalty to his paper and loyalty to his friends were the two strong characteristics in Harry Weldon's make-up.

When the news was flashed over the country that Harry Weldon has been stricken with paralysis, thousands felt a personal shock. Particularly so was this true in Cincinnati, and all of his friends were gladly ready to render him every assistance that was within their power.

Thousands of letters of sympathy were received from all parts of the country, paying a glowing tribute to the prince of good fellows, and expressing their best wishes for his speedy recovery.

He was then taken to Circleville, Ohio, his old home, where, under the careful nursing of faithful friends, he was given every comfort until his end came some months afterwards. Morris H. Isaacs, for whom Harry Weldon expressed the greatest friendship, was sent for the morning of his illness, and he remained with Harry for three weeks, never leaving his bedside in all that time.

In April of 1900, it was suggested by Morris H. Isaacs that a subscription be started to relieve his old friend of any anxiety as to his future financial condition. The announcement was made through

The Harry Weldon Fund Committee. Charles Hodges; Morris H. Isaacs; Judge Howard Ferris; Ren Mulford, Jr.; Wm. Lowlow, Jr.; Amor Smith, Jr.; Dan Murphy; Joseph Nolan; J. Ed. Grillo.

the columns of the *Enquirer*, when contributions began to pour in from every state in the Union, while persons in France, England and Australia responded to personal letters written them by Mr. Isaacs. Not only the lovers of baseball, but the sporting fraternity in general came to the front.

The first contribution was given by Ben Greenwald, of Cincinnati, who started the fund with $50.00; the late William J. O'Dell (the well-known broker), signed his check for $500.00, which Mr. Isaacs made out for him, Mr. O'Dell stating that he would sign for whatever amount Mr. Isaacs should choose. The others who followed shortly to the aid of their old friend were:

R.T. Holloway, Saratoga Springs, N.Y $100.00
E.W. Baylis, Stag Cafe............................100.00
Andy Gilligan 100.00
George C. Bennett, Chicago 100.00
Charles (Kid) McCoy, New York 50.00
Robert J. O'Brien 50.00
Col. Dacy, Norwood Inn 100.00
W.H. Busted, New York 100.00
Theodore Foucar 25.00
Ban B. Johnson, Chicago 25.00
Barney Dreyfuss, Pittsburg 25.00
James Keenan... 25.00
John J. Ryan 25.00
Samuel R. Brown, Pittsburg 25.00
A.J. Reach, Philadelphia 25.00

The above were received within two days after the announcement in the paper, after which hundreds of others followed. The total amount contributed was an exceedingly neat sum.

Mr. Isaacs then proposed giving a benefit day at the ball park to swell the benefit sum, which occurred on Saturday, October 6, 1900. This was surely a red letter day in the history of local sport, long to be remembered. Mr. Isaacs was assisted in his undertakings by Judge Howard Ferris, one of the staunchest friends the Cincinnati ball players ever had. A committee was appointed to make the necessary arrangements to carry out the program of the day, which consisted of the following:

Chairman .... Judge Howard Ferris
Vice-President.. M.E. Moch

Base Ball in Cincinnati

From photo taken at the time. The Cincinnati Newspaper Baseball Club.
Champions of 1895. George A. Holmes; Charles H. Zuber; Wm. E.
Owens; Chas. J. Christie. Geo. A. Townsend, Jr.; Jas. W. Faulkner;
George S. McDowell; Harry Shafer; Webb Melbourne; Ed. H. Anthony;
Kent Loomis.

Second Vice-President .... John H. Allen
Third Vice-President .... Judge William Jackson
Treasurer.................................... Hon. Julius Fleischmann
Secretary................................... Morris H. Isaacs

The celebration started at 12:30 P.M., with a large street parade,
in which participated the following:

Patrol Wagons.
Mounted Police.

Chapter XI

One company of police in command of Acting Chief Casey
and Major Carroll.

First Regiment Band, led by Major George G. Smith.

Walnut Hills Cadets.

Actors in tallyhos.

Fire Trustees in carriages.

City Council and visiting officials in carriages.

Amateur players in carriages.

House of Refuge Cadets.

The Zoo animals.

At the ball park athletic contests preceded the game of the afternoon. John O'Brien of the Twos' Fire Engine Company, carried off the prize in the 100-yard dash, in 12 seconds; Ed. Brendamour and John Zettel gave a ten-minute wrestling match; Tom Parrott won the long-distance throw, sending the ball over the field a distance of 352 feet; the Y.M.C.A. took the prize in the relay race.

The ball game was then played between the local newspaper men and the actors who were performing at the various theaters at the time. The line-up was as follows:

NEWSPAPER MEN.

Chas. J. Christie, Sec'y to the Mayor .... Third Base
James W. Faulkner, of the *Enquirer* .... Second Base
Ed. Grillo, of the *Commercial Tribune* .... First Base
Donald Dunbar, of the *Post* .... Center Field
Sam Assur, of the *Commercial Tribune* .... Pitcher
Hubbard Schwartz, of the *Times-Star* .... Right Field
Moses Strauss, of the *Times-Star*......................... Catcher
Bo Needham, of the *Detroit Free Press* .... Shortstop
Theodore Mitchell, of the *Enquirer* .... Left Field

Base Ball in Cincinnati

ACTORS.

Gaylor .... Shortstop
Genaro .... Left Field
Fuller .... Third Base
Irving .... Catcher
Goodwin .... Pitcher
Morris .... Center Field
MacIntoch .... Second Base
White .... Right Field

But three innings were played, and the score was:

Innings	1	2	3	
Newspaper	0	0	0	—0
Actors	2	0	2	—4

Judge Howard Ferris, the master of ceremonies, and Judge Aaron McNeil were the umpires.

The amount realized from the subscriptions and from the receipts of the game was the handsome sum of $10,300. This was turned over to the Weldon Fund Committee, which was composed of Judge Howard Ferris, Chairman; Julius Fleischmann, Treasurer; Morris H. Isaacs, Amor Smith, Jr., Charles Hodges, Dan Murphy, Ren Mulford, Jr., William Lowlow, Joe Nolan and Ed. Grillo. On March 9, 1901, this committee went to Circleville, Ohio, the home of Harry Weldon, and performed the pleasant task of presenting Harry with a check on the Market National Bank, signed by Julius Fleischmann as Treasurer of the Weldon Fund Committee, for $10,300.

Many eloquent tributes were paid the stricken man by Judge Howard Ferris, Amor Smith and others, who spoke on the occasion of the presentation, but one who was deserving of virtually all the credit for the success of the beneficial undertaking was not overlooked.

Morris H. Isaacs was justly praised for his loyal friendship to Mr. Weldon.

His devotion was splendidly dwelt upon by Judge Howard Ferris, who was in a better position than any one else to know of Mr. Isaacs' tireless efforts to make the fund as large as possible.

Judge Howard Ferris, as chairman of the committee, among other things said, in presenting the check: "Your friends learned of your great misfortune with sorrow, and their affection and regard for you has taken a very tangible form. With their desire to show their appreciation of you as a man and the interest you have taken in the elevation of matters connected with athletic sports, they began what has been, ever since its inception, a labor of

From a recent photo. Judge Howard Ferris, An Old-time Player. A Staunch Friend of the Cincinnati Ball Players.

love, and when it was known that an avenue had been provided through which they could express their regard for you, contributions came from all parts of the country, with letters from donors that deserve to be handed down to posterity.... We know that you will receive this mark of esteem and friendship in the spirit in which it has been given; that you will accept it as another evidence of the high regard and favor in which every one holds you. We wish you godspeed and a long and successful life."

The committee returned to Cincinnati the next day, feeling joyful over the task they had performed.

THE WEDDING AT THE HOME PLATE—FIRST DIAMOND WEDDING RECORD.

League Park has been the scene of many notable fete days, and ranking with the most unique was a wedding at the home plate, that took place at the Western Avenue grounds on September 18, 1893. It was the first and only time that Cupid and Hymen ever found a battery for the earliest matrimonial innings on a ball field.

Frank Bancroft was the sponsor for this remarkable affair. The name of Bancroft is written indelibly upon the pages of American history, and the name of Frank C. Bancroft is woven in the woof of Cincinnati baseball history.

The groom in this baseball wedding was one of the famous duo of ball ground attaches known to sporting fame as the "Can Brothers." When the story of the coming wedding of the head of the firm came out, Frank Bancroft offered League Park for the nuptials, and his proposition was accepted. The ceremony prefaced the game in which Tom Parrott succeeded Charlie King at the slab, and the Reds beat the Baltimores 7 to 6. The bleachers were packed on this occasion, and when the bridal party appeared at the gates—the affair took place on the old diamond and before the Palace of the Fans was built—a welcoming shout greeted them. They were driven across the field in carriages. At second base they alighted, and the march that was to end at the rubber began. Commodore Tyrell, the chief justice of Avenue Nine, stepped out from the maddening throng to meet them. In all his career as the marrying squire he had had no such experience as this. The bridal party was well bunched, with Louis

Rapp, the groom, putting his best foot forward and smiling upon the populace.

Upon the lapel of the coat of the Red's assistant groundkeeper rested a big boutonniere, and, as the ovation continued, Louis waved his white gloved hand to the crowd, and, quivering there in the air, it looked like a bolt of muslin. Louis was superlatively joyful. Miss Rose Smith and her maids, Clara Frank and Hannah Moeller, were attired in white. The groomsmen were George Frank and Al Johnson. The home plate had been covered with linen, and a half a dozen tiny flags held the white carpeting in place. The commodore tied the nuptial knot in fast time. To the left the Reds and the Baltimores were grouped, and after George Tyrrell had presented the scroll which certified that two more hearts were beating as one, Captain Latham, in behalf of the Reds, presented a handsome purse, and the Baltimores followed suit.

The Cincinnati club's gift was a chamber suit, while there were innumerable other presents. Mingled with the shower of rice which fell around them were many silver coins. Some fan, in a spirit of mischief, tossed out a doll baby, which Louis gathered in, tucking it under his arm with a grin, but the bride gave the offending doll a jerk and tossed it away. It fell and broke its neck, while the multitude roared.

From a recent photo. Frank C. Bancroft, *Business Manager*, CINCINNATI BASEBALL CLUB.

The Wedding at the Home Plate.

Returning to their carriages, the party drove out, circling past the bleachers, where the coatless sun gods shouted their farewells. For the first time on record the circus seats were invaded by the fair sex, and the afternoon that saw the first bride of the diamond gave the nosy clan the only "queens of the bleachers" that they have ever known.

As the carriages rolled out of the grounds, Col. Deutsch Oehler fired off a cannon at first base, and out in the Queen & Crescent yards an engine whistled good luck to the couple.

After the game and the crowd had gone, a young man, whose buried chin hung down over his boiled shirt, leaned disconsolately against a silent turnstile, a veritable chromo of woe in best bib and tucker. It was "Snooks." With a sigh that rumbled along toward the distant heights of Mount Harrison, he simply said: "The old firm of Can Brothers is busted at last."

FIELD DAY AT LEAGUE PARK.

Wednesday, September 11, 1907, marks an epoch in the history of baseball in Cincinnati. On that day was held at the League Park what was called Bowlers' Field Day, when the first records for baseball field events were made before one of the most enthusiastic as well as the largest week day crowds that ever attended any game at League Park, and the affair proved itself to be intensely interesting from start to finish.

The program of the day began at 1:30 P.M. with a concert by Weber's Band. At 2:15 there was a fancy wand drill exercise by the class of the North Cincinnati Turn-Verein, under the direction of Prof. N.C. Seuss, and at 2:30 began baseball field events, when $100.00 in gold and a suitable medal properly inscribed was awarded to the winner in each event. The events which were run off and the winners of each were as follows:

Long Distance Fungo Hitting—Mike Mitchell, of Cincinnati. Distance, 413 feet 8½ inches.

Accurate Throwing—George Gibson, of Pittsburg.

Running Out a Fair Bunt to First Base—John Thoney, of Toronto. Time, 3 1-5 seconds.

Long Distance Throwing—Sheldon LeJeune, Springfield, Ohio. Distance, 399 feet 10-¾ inches.

Circling the Bases—W.O. Clements, of Jersey City. Time, 14 1-5 seconds.

After these events followed a game between the Cincinnati and the Pittsburg Clubs. Owing to the lateness of the afternoon it was decided to play only five innings, but as the score stood a tie at the end of the five innings, two more were played, which resulted in a victory for the Cincinnati team in a score of 2 to 1.

The officials of the day were:

Referee—W.M. Rankin, of New York City.
Judges—Clyde Johnson, Harry C. Pulliam and John E. Bruce.
Starter—Starbuck Smith.
Timers—M.C. Longenecker, E.W. Murphy, and Tom Andrews, Milwaukee, Wis.
Measurers—Prof. Al Brodbeck, Prof. N.C. Seuss, and Ed. Brendamour.
Clerk of the Course—Morris H. Isaacs.
Scorer—Ren Mulford, Jr.

JAMES W. HOLLIDAY BENEFIT.

James W. ("Bug") Holliday, once a fine center fielder in the Cincinnati nine during the eighties, had retired from the field and had engaged in some other business. His health afterwards began to fail, and, being in straitened circumstances, his friends decided to give him a benefit at League Park. On Saturday, September 14, 1907, two games of ball were played and the proceeds of the day, which was a good sum, were given to "Bug."

The first game played was between the Hyde Park and the Queen City Athletic Club teams, which resulted in a score of 6 to 0 in favor of the Queen City boys. The second game was between the old-time Reds and the Pen and Pencil team, which was composed

The Cincinnati Baseball Park, Showing Grand Stand.

of the members of the press, who fell easy victims to the prowess of the old stars who were lined up against them, in a score of 10 to 2.

THE OLD-TIME REDS.

Sommers .... Third Base
Schwartz.. Right Field
McPhee .... Second Base
Mullane .... Shortstop
Stenzel.. Center Field
Reilly .... First Base
Keenan .... Catcher
Boyle .... Left Field
Shallix .... Pitcher
Hahn .... Pitcher

Base Ball in Cincinnati

THE PEN AND PENCIL NINE.

Goss .... Center Field and Third Base
Bashman .... First Base and Catcher
Aultman .... Left Field
Schribley...................................... Catcher and First Base
Dahlman .... Second Base
Joyce .... Third Base and Center Field
Potter... Right Field
Cook.. Shortstop
Sprengard .... Pitcher
Bushelman .... Pitcher and Shortstop

The umpire of the game was Jack Breuer.

The present officers of the Cincinnati Baseball Club are:

Hon. August Herrmann .... President
Col. Max C. Fleischmann.................. Secretary-Treasurer

THE DIRECTORS.

Hon. August Herrmann.
Col. Max C. Fleischmann.
Hon. Julius Fleischmann.
Casper H. Rowe.
John C. Gallagher.

Redland history would be incomplete without a reference to the good work of John G. Reilly, John Corkhill, Jim Keenan, Tony Mullane, Billy Rhines, Charles Jones, Gus Shallix, Tom Mansell, Ren Deagle, Jimmy Peoples, George Tebeau, "Germany" Smith, Jerry Harrington, Frank Dwyer, Phil Ehret, Elmer Smith, Kid Baldwin, Jim White, Lip Pike, Bug Holliday, Jake Beckley, Hugh Nicol, Lee Viau, Harry Vaughn, Frank Foreman, Frank Hahn, and a host of others, some of whom have slid across the home plate of eternity, while the rest are still playing life's game.

Index

Compiled by the Editors

Index

Index

Index

Index

Index

Index

Forest Citys *see* Cleveland, OH, clubs; Rockford, IL, clubs
Foster, A.H. 78
Foster, I.D. 78
Foucar, Theodore 187
France, W. 78
Francisco 48
Frank, Clara 193
Frank, George 193
Franklin, A. 78
Frazer, E.S. 78
Freeman, Dr. Z. 78
Freeman Avenue, Cincinnati 26
Freeman Street, Cincinnati 57
French, Salsbury 52, 129
Frost, Theodore 19, 20, 21
Fuller 190
Fulmer, Charles "Chick" 170, 178

Gaddis, T.C. 80
Gaff, C.C. 80
Gaff, J.W. 80
Galbreath, R.H. 80
Gallagher, John C. 198
Gamble, James N. 80
Gamble, W.A. 80
Garlick 86
Garner 181
Garrigan, Michael A. 36, 88
Gaylor 190
Gazlay, Carter 80, 111, 113
Genaro 190
George, Dick 48, 52
Gerke, George 170
Gerling, Louis 66
Getty, Frank 80
Gibson, George 195
Gibson, W.D. 18
Gibson House 103, 109, 111, 116, 178
Gilligan, Andy 187
Gillmore, C. 80
Gladden, James 43, 127
Gladiators *see* Cincinnati, OH, clubs

Glassford, Henry A. 24, 25, 69, 78
Glendales *see* Cincinnati, OH, clubs
Glover 144
Golden 48
Goldsmith, Fred 170
Goodhue, G.W. 80
Goodman, W. Austin 23, 34, 80
Goodwin 190
Goshorn, Alfred T. 23, 24, 25, 78, 84, 90, 91, 93, 102, 112
Goshorn, E.C. 78
Goss 198
Gothams *see* Hoboken, NY, clubs
Gould 136, 138, 139, 140, 143
Gould, Charles A. 46, 48, 53
Gould, Charles H. 18, 19, 36, 37, 60, 64, 80, 94, 95, 99, 114, 119, 121, 136, 138, 139, 140, 143, 158, 178
Graham 86
Grant 30
Grant, James B. 78
Grant, Moses 22, 33, 53, 61, 64, 78
Grant, Richard 86
Grant, President Ulysses S. 84, 110, 112
Grant, W. 22
Gray, Bill 178, 182
Great Westerns *see* Cincinnati, OH, clubs; Mansfield, OH, clubs
Green, L.A. 78
Greenwald, Ben 186
Greenwood, William 50, 80
Gregg, Oscar 80
Gregg, Theodore E. 80
Greggs, E.H. 32
Griffith, C.P. 78
Griffith, Griffith P. 68, 78
Griffith, John 43
Griffith, Joseph 48, 52, 89
Griffith, W.S. 68, 78
Grillo, J. Ed. 181, 186, 189, 190
Groesbeck, W.S. 80
Guild, Frank 68
Guild, Harry 68

Index

Index

Index

Index

Neave, James L. 81
Neave, Thomas, Jr. 81
Neave, William P. 81
Needham, Bo 189
Neff, George W. 81
Neff, J. Wayne 24, 33, 50, 81, 125, 173
Neff, M.P. 81
Neff, Peter Rudolph 81
Neff, William H. 81
Neiman 46
Netter, G. 81
New Brunswick, NJ, Libertys 13
New England League 168
New Haven, CT, Yales [Yale College] 104, 130
New Orleans, LA, clubs: Atlantics 149; Lone Stars 125, 149; Pelicans 125, 149; Robert E. Lees 149; Southerns 118, 125, 149
New York, NY 15, 16, 32, 43, 108, 115, 158, 177, 187, 196
New York, NY, clubs: Actives 105, 130; Baltics 13; Champions 13; Empires 144; Giants 175; Gothams 100; Harlems 13; Independents 13; Knickerbockers 8, 9, 11, 12, 13, 15, 26, 94; Metropolitans 13, 173; Mutuals 72, 73, 94, 99, 100, 104, 105, 106, 107, 116, 117, 118, 130, 131, 132, 133, 134, 135, 149, 150; "New York Club" 8, 9
New York Clipper 54, 64, 73, 133
New York Clipper Medal 58
New York Cricket Club 26
New York League 168
Newark, NJ, clubs: Amateurs 149; Newarks 13
Newhall, J. DeS. 81
Newlin, Major 66
Newport, KY, Holts 30, 40, 41, 42; junior nine 128
Niagaras *see* Buffalo, NY, clubs
Nichols, A.H. 172
Nicol, Hugh 198

Noble, Will P. 81, 147, 155
Nolan, Joseph 186, 190
Northern-Copper Country League 168
Northwestern League 168
Norton, Len 81
Norton, Major 67
Norton, T. 39
Noyes, E.F. 81, 113
Nutt, William 89

Oakley, W.A. 81
O'Brien, John 189
O'Brien, Robert J. 187
Occidentals *see* Quincy, IL, Occidentals
O'Connell, Dan 50
O'Dell, William J. 186
O'Donnel, T.D. 81
O'Dowd, M. 36, 46, 88
Oehler, Col. Deutsch 194
Ogden, W.J. 18
Ohio Association 38–40
Ohio-Pennsylvania League 168
Ohio-Pennsylvania-Maryland League 168
Old Elms *see* Pittsfield, MA, Old Elms
Olympics *see* Philadelphia, PA, clubs; Washington, DC, clubs; Pittsburg, PA, clubs
Omaha, NE, clubs: Omahas 118; Otoes 118
Omahas *see* Omaha, NE, clubs
O'Neill, Tip 173
Ontarios *see* Oswego, NY, Ontarios
Orientals *see* Memphis, TN, Orientals
Orioles *see* Baltimore, MD, clubs
Orions *see* Lexington, KY, Orions
Osceolas *see* Cincinnati, OH, clubs
O'Shaughnessy, J.H. 81
O'Shaughnessy, Louis 81
Oswego, NY, Ontarios 129, 149
Otoes *see* Omaha, NE, clubs
Outcalt, Miller 44, 45, 47, 89
Owen, William 81, 188

Index

Index

Radcliff, J. 140, 141, 143
Railway Unions *see* Cleveland, OH, clubs; Columbus, OH, clubs
Ralfey 52
Rammelsberg, Charles 82
Rammelsberg, Oscar 43, 44
Ramp, Samuel W. 68, 69, 82
Ranch Tales of the Rockies 2
Randolph, J.F. 82
Rankin, William M. 162, 196
Ransick 181
Rapp, Louis 192–193
Ravens *see* Cincinnati, OH, clubs
Reach, Al 140, 141, 144, 187
Reckel, C. 40
Record 129
Red Hooks *see* Cincinnati, OH, clubs
Red Hots *see* Cincinnati, OH, clubs
Red Stockings *see* Cincinnati Reds
Redlegs *see* Cincinnati Reds
Reds *see* Cincinnati Reds
"The Reds of Sixty-Nine" (lyric) 120
Reed, Thomas 86
Reilly, John G. "Long John" 178, 197, 198
Reliables *see* Covington, KY, Reliables
Republics *see* Columbus, OH, clubs
Resolutes *see* Cincinnati, OH, clubs; Elizabeth, NJ, Resolutes; Hamilton, OH, Resolutes
Resor, Charles H. 51, 82
Resor, Frank 82
Resor, I. Burnet 26, 82
Resor, William, Jr. 26, 82
Rhines, Billy 182, 198
Rianhard, W.E. 82
Richards 48
Richardson 30
Richey, R.W. 69
Richter, Francis 3
Ridgeway, W.S. 66, 82
Ringwalt, R. 82, 125
Riversides *see* Cincinnati, OH, clubs; Portsmouth, OH, Riversides

Robert E. Lees *see* New Orleans, LA, clubs
Rochester, NY, clubs: Alerts 104, 117, 118; Flour Citys 129
Rockford, IL, Forest Citys 89, 113, 118, 122, 123, 146, 148, 150
Rogers 127
Rogers, Fraley V. 154
Rogers, John I. 165
Rogers, R.F. 82
Roll, Ad. R. 43
Rollins, F.H. 82
Rollwagen, L. 39
Romer 181
Root, James 31
Rorer, J.W. 21
Ross 59
Roth, Frank 43, 44
Rounders 5, 7
Rowe, Casper H. 175, 198
Rudel 181
Ruffin, Chief 115
Ryan 37
Ryan, James 31
Ryan, John J. 187
Ryan, W.W. 38

St. Johns, J.H. 40
St. Louis, MO, clubs: Browns (AA) 173, 174; Browns (AL) 166; Empires 116, 118, 150; Unions 71, 89, 116, 118, 150
St. Nicholas Club *see* Hoboken, NJ, clubs
St. Xavier's College 87
San Francisco, CA, clubs: Atlantics 116, 118; Eagles 116, 118; Pacifics 116, 118
Sanderson 129
Sands, George F. 17, 18, 32, 38, 39, 52
Santmyer, J.P. 82
Sayler, Milton 82
Scanlan, Charles S. 69, 82
Scarrit, J.A. 52

Index

Index

Tucker, William 9
Tudor, "Tave" 69
Tudor, Octavius H. 19, 24, 82
Tudor, Thomas H. 82
Turner 30
Tusculum 128
Two Old Cat 5, 8
Tyrrell, George 192, 193

Ulmer, Charles 46
Union Association 164, 170
Union Cricket Club 24, 26, 27
Unions *see* Lansingburg, NY, Unions;
   Morrisania, NY, Unions; St. Louis,
   MO, Unions; Urbana, OH, Unions
Unions of Haymakers [sic] *see* Lans-
   ingburg, NY, Unions
Urbana, OH, Unions 127, 149
Urner, Henry C. 83

Van, Chas. 48
Van Buren, James H. 86
Van Loo, Leon 83
Van Valkenberg, H. 69, 83
Van Voorhis, G.H. 158
Vandergrift, George 83
Vaughn, Harry 182, 198
Viau, Lee 198
Virginia League 168
Von Phul, H. 51

Wachman, D. 83
Wagner, Honus 171
Wald 181
Walker, C.S. 83
Walker, Charles 105, 130
Walker, Edward W. 43, 52, 85, 89
Walker, J.H. 83
Walker, Smiley 43, 129
Walnut Hills *see* Cincinnati, OH, clubs
Walnut Hills, OH, Pickwicks (junior
   nine) 46, 47
Walters 129
Ward, John Montgomery 162

Warfield, J. 83
Washington, DC, clubs: Nationals 29,
   40, 55, 72, 94, 100, 110, 114, 117, 122,
   123, 150, 165; Olympics 40, 72, 110,
   117, 118, 150, 153; Senators (AL) 166
Washington Court House, OH, Ama-
   teurs 150
Wasson, B.W. 83
Waterman, Fred 53, 54, 61, 64, 68, 83,
   94, 95, 100, 114, 119, 120, 125, 136, 137,
   140, 143
Watkins, W.H. 174
Watson, Robert 127
Watson, William E. 126, 127
Wayne, J.L., Jr. 83
Weatherhead, R.H. 83
Webb, J.A. 83
Wehmer, George 18
Welch, Curt 173
Weldon, Harry 190, 191
Weldon Fund Committee 190
Wells, Charles 51
Welsch 38
Wentworth, E. 83
Werner, George 66
Westen Association 165, 168
Western Canada League 168
Western League 168
Western Pennsylvania League 168
Westerns *see* Indianapolis, IA, clubs
Wheaton, William R. 9
Wheeler, Harry 170, 176, 183
Wheeling, WV, Baltics 71, 110, 117
Wheelright, Thomas 48
Whetstone, Albert 49
Whetstone, John C. 83
White 190
White, D.A. 83
White, J.M. 39
White, Jim 198
White, Will 178
White, William H. 170
White Oak, OH, junior nine 128

Index